The Last Lost Warrior

Tom A Preece

DEDICATION

In memory of three wonderful friends,
Steve, Floyd, and George,
All United States Marines who survived Vietnam.
All died young,
And that is not a coincidence.

For the Infantry now and always

ACKNOWLEDGMENTS

First of course my wife, Diane, for her patience, support, editing, and proof reading.

Special thanks to my volunteer editors, Jinx McCombs along with Steve and Carol Chell. They all probed more than grammar and usage, noted distortions of nuance and provided character advice.

The Wednesday session of my Community garden at The Sea Ranch, The Posh Squash, were my first beta readers and provided vigorous advice.

The Book Group With No Rules, (who I have been reading with since 1995 or so,) also read and critiqued a quite early draft.

Dan Wormhoudt and Leslie Hoppe also served as beta readers, and were perhaps my most enthusiastic cheerleaders throughout the refinement process.

Four special women, not only Beta readers but fabulous support: Harrie Alley, Wendi Maxwell, Deborah Francis Ames, and Vaden Riggs.

The late Marge Harrison taught me to love literature and how to recognize a good sentence.

Rowdy Harrington tramping The Sea Ranch trails with our dogs, Huck and Caleb, taught me much about structure and character.

Special thanks to Recon 1/7th vet Bruce Leonard who seems to have fought in Vietnam and every war since. Bruce is an expert in small arms who pointed out to me that I couldn't silence a .357 Magnum, and provided a detailed description of the construction of Alpha Alpha or Automatic Ambush which is featured in this story. I had long since forgotten how to make one.

Special thanks to Conrad M. Leighton who photographed the members of E Recon 1/7th Cavalry, 1st Air Cavalry Division and then asked me to find them - which I did. That journey was an important emotional source for this novel. I gratefully recommend Conrad's own book:

"War Stories, A GI Reporter in Vietnam, 1970-1971"

Cover Creation by Jeff Raby. of Creatis Group Inc.

CHAPTER 1

May 6, 2006

Maybe I'd never had it so good; maybe not.

I knew guys who thought I had it made. As a retired cop I had a good pension; I kept busy and entertained by my PI business, but not so much it felt like work. I lived in pleasant surroundings among good friends; I ate well; I indulged myself in craft beer and occasional whiskey. I had money enough for me and mine for life.

Today I sat above the third base line of the Oakland Coliseum high enough to stay shaded in the afternoon sun, the perfect spot to watch the A's infield double plays. Zito was pitching.

I was supposed to be having a good time, but wasn't. I had the jumps; my shrink tells me I'm hyper alert. Didn't matter that I knew why; I kept looking over my shoulder and was startled at every sudden motion at the edge of sight.

When my cell phone rang, I looked first, saw the Milwaukee area code, 414, and knew who called.

"What do you want, El Tee?" I said without preamble.

"Not so much," he said. "I wanted to update you on the new guys I've found. Maybe chat a little. Reminisce."

"Uh huh," I said. "There would also be a new date proposal for your reunion. And you've maybe spotted the one armed man who's after us again. I'm at a ball park on a fine spring day. I'd just as soon you didn't fuck that up. Don't call me back," I said as I hung up the phone..

He started my nightmares. Or maybe he had just raked them up. I still had the jumps. Whatever trouble was coming the El Tee's phone call wasn't it. I'm a combat veteran, a former grunt, in Vietnam a squad leader in a Recon platoon. I had trained for much of my young life to smell trouble coming. Last year my El Tee, my Lieutenant platoon leader in the bush, had found me.

When he first called me, I was pretty shocked.

The second and third time he called we had a lot of laughs.

Later not so much. He was on about getting Tuco and me to a reunion with Recon. I thought he should have known we could never do that, but then maybe he wasn't in his right mind.

He'd become paranoid. He thought the CID was after us 30 years after the fact. Each of Recon's random human encounters seemed to the El Tee to be new evidence of a vague persecution that made no sense to Tuco, me, or Lily.

Until the El Tee found us, I had dreamed of Vietnam only sometimes. After his phone calls turned dark and conspiratorial, I had not only dreams, but terrifying nightmares. One intruded badly on my reality.

I woke in the middle of the night, drenched with sweat, my hands bearing down and squeezing Lily's throat. I had to leave, not, as I told her, because I didn't love her, but because I did.

She didn't buy it. She called me chicken.

Maybe I was just cautious. I got out of the house and moved into the cottage behind the house of my USMC buddy, Floyd.

I tried to watch Zito pitch in my distracted state when the phone rang again. It wasn't the El Tee this time, but, Bob Schooner.

"You sent Tuco to see me a couple of months ago?"

"Yeah," I said.

"I gotta show you something."

"Will I want to see it?" I asked.

2

"Probably not. I'm at the Contra Costa County morgue. Can you come out?"

"I'm at the Coliseum," I said. "I took B.A.R.T. Can you pick me up at Pleasant Hill?"

"I'll put the game on," he said. "This isn't urgent. I'll meet you when it's over."

A corpse was trouble enough. I quit looking for more, relaxed and watched the game. The A's won.

Glowery was the one reason Schooner would want me at the morgue, not his body of course – we should be so lucky. More than likely it was someone Schooner thought Glowery killed.

Schooner's an undercover. Normally I wouldn't know, but twenty years ago "Ghost" Glowery decided to move in on me, bought a house in my town, El Sobrante, and become a model citizen. Since he was the only serious hood I knew, I took it as a personal challenge, but I couldn't touch him. The crime rate in his neighborhood went down, probably because it was well patrolled by fat guys on motor bikes. Glowery was a notorious drug trafficker, the general for an army of biker thugs. For the sake of my own political skin I explained to my city council and other law enforcement leaders, that I, George Duvall, El Sobrante's Chief of Police, knew Glowery personally.

Tuco, "Ghost" Glowery, and I all served in the same Recon platoon in Vietnam. When Schooner went on the street specifically to get intel on Glowery's thugs, he decided he needed to talk to Tuco and me. Otherwise I would never have met him; Tuco would never have met him, or even known who he was.

Some would call this coincidence; I don't. Tuco and I were tethered to each other long ago watching each other's back. I could guess at Ghost's motives, though I don't understand them. In Nam he was walking graceful death, killing the enemy anyway he could and always mystified that he was not in charge. I had been a squad leader; he was not. I had become the Chief of Police in El Sobrante; he had become notorious thug. I think he moved to El Sobrante to make a move on me.

At the Pleasant Hill station I made eye contact with Schooner as I fed my ticket through the exit machine. He gave his head a negative shake and walked off into the parking lot while I followed, one aisle over and fifty feet back. If he had a tail it wasn't close, and in the parking lot I think you'd have to be following closely or lose him once he got to his car.

He climbed in the driver's seat of a black sedan. I passed him, still an aisle over, pulled out my own car keys and cut between parked cars as if I was going for the car next to him, but got in his passenger door.

"Aren't we being a little paranoid?" I asked.

"Just cautious. I wouldn't want anybody to wonder why a guy who looks like me is a friend of a guy who looks like you."

Bob has shoulder length hair going gray. His Fu Manchu mustache brushes his collar. He was wearing biker boots, a sweatshirt with a denim vest and jeans. I still look like a police chief though I've been retired a couple of years.

"I see the point," I said.

At the morgue Schooner had a gate pass for the secure parking lot and the doors of the morgue. The attendant gave him a key and the drawer number.

"Thanks," Bob said. We walked into the pathologist's surgery.

"Before I open this drawer," he said, "I've got to warn you what you'll see won't be pretty."

"It never is," I said.

Someone had pounded a baseball into the dead guy's mouth. His lips had been sliced off. There was a sheet over the rest of the body. Bob put on a pair of sterile gloves and pulled it back to expose everything.

"He's more off color than usual," Bob said. They found him in the Delta and he'd been underwater a long time."

"Did you find the genitals," I asked.

"No. They're probably in the belly of a Delta catfish. He died ugly, tortured way past what was needed to make him talk."

"You know the motive?"

4

"Not really. The torture was done slowly, inflicting pain not likely to kill. Here, take a look."

He held up the corpse's hand. There were three holes in it, through and through.

"According to the M.E. and the crime lab, they nailed him down to something wooden. There are splinters embedded all over his back. They kept nailing, aiming carefully to stay away from the blood supply, just trying to drive nails through bone. It took a long time."

I reached for my barf bag, but didn't lose it.

"Maybe they didn't want him to talk. Maybe it was just punishment."

"The shrinks don't think so," Schooner said. "It was done with great deliberation and obsessive planning. There's forensic evidence of more than one guy in the act, but clearly there was a sadistic sociopath controlling it all. The first pains were intense but did little damage. They were meant to make him talk. The damage was increased slowly by someone who knew how and enjoyed it. Only then near the point of death was he punished with the castration and the baseball. He died in hours not in minutes."

He draped the corpse, closed the drawer and locked it.

"And you think this is Glowery's work," I said.

"Don't you remember, Duvall? Eight years ago? Almost exactly the same MO. We just couldn't get enough to nail him for it, no pun intended."

"Glowery's not my business anymore," I said. "I'm retired.

"You called me a couple of months ago," he said. "You said you had Tuco chasing down a missing person, a certain Keith Newton. You wanted to know if he had any beef with the law. I found only an old assault, nothing much; he got off on probation. When this body showed up I remembered your call.

"This body used to be Keith Newton. This is the guy Tuco was looking for. Now we're looking for Tuco," Schooner said. "Glowery's looking too. And maybe looking for you."

"Huh?"

"Guys on the street know I'm a vet. One of Glowery's apprentice gang bangers asked did I know a guy from a 1st Cav Recon platoon." Schooner grinned and raised an eyebrow.

"So what did you tell him?"

"I said sure, George Duvall, the retired top cop in El Sobrante. He kinda lost interest."

"You didn't mention Tuco."

"I thought Tuco might be in trouble. Now he's gummed up in a murder investigation. But don't worry. Nobody thinks he did it."

I nodded. Maybe not this time.

"But you want to talk to him?" I asked.

"Not exactly," Schooner said. "I want you to talk to him."

"You or me? What's the difference?" I asked. "I'll be in touch as soon as he gets back in town. He owes me a report for my files."

"I guess you don't know. Tuco's been back and left again about a month ago. I talked to Lily."

"Oh."

"We think he's hiding out," Schooner said. "We know Glowery's looking for him, and I'd bet that Tuco knows. But we only know about Tuco because Tuco talked to me."

"That would be the royal coply 'we'?" I asked. "You'd be the only one who knew about Tuco."

"Yeah, until I talked this over with my Lieutenant. Glowery's after Tuco. Tuco knows it, but Glowery don't know that we know about Tuco. Maybe it's better if he don't"

"So you don't want to look for Tuco directly." I said. "You want me to do it. If I file a missing person report and nose around, I'm just a concerned employer and friend, and maybe nothing to do with Glowery."

"Exactly," Schooner said. "Just keep me informed. I'll relay the pertinent stuff to the investigators through my Lieutenant but I won't be using your name. Even if the department leaks, Glowery will never know it's you."

"Not the way I would do it. The murder book won't get my raw observations. You're a filter even if you don't know it. You'll miss something."

"Doesn't matter what you want," Schooner said. "My El Tee. says that's what Tommy wants, and it's our jurisdiction."

Tommy was my old colleague, Tommy Howard, the Contra Costa Sheriff. The Delta sprawls between four counties, and apparently the body turned up on Contra Costa.

"Have it your way," I said. "I'll keep you in the loop."

"You could start by telling me about this missing person case," Schooner said.

"Not much to tell," I said. "I'll tell you what I know.

"Newton was old friend of Tuco's. A woman therapist they both knew asked Tuco to find him. Newton, the former patient of the client, had gone missing again. He screwed up his life a long time ago. Years ago his kid committed suicide, and that broke him. His marriage broke up and he took a long trip through candy land before the woman helped him. Now he's suicidal again. He's saying goodbye to old friends. Apparently Tuco got him out of a similar jam years ago. He said the shrink wanted to talk to Newton one more time and a cell phone call would be enough."

"Did you know, Newton?" Bob asked.

"No."

"Tuco's your best bud going back years but you didn't know this good friend?"

"Yeah, I know. I should have noticed. I got too caught up trying to manage the client. I told Tuco we shouldn't take the case because of the suicide angle. Maybe he could find Newton. Maybe we could get him to call her. No matter what, she probably expected us to save him. We couldn't guarantee that."

"So why'd you take it?"

"He said it would be a lifetime favor."

"A lifetime favor huh?"

"Ever watch White Christmas?" I asked.

"Bing Crosby and Danny Kaye?"

"Yeah. There's a lot of places where Danny Kaye grabs his arm and flinches to remind Crosby that Kaye broke his arm during the war saving Crosby," I said.

"I remember."

"Always makes me think of me and Tuco. He doesn't flinch. There's no clowning around. I still think I owe him, and that's probably why I let him take this case," I said.

"This time he's in a lot of trouble," Schooner said.

"Nothing new," I said. "Can you drive me home?"

CHAPTER 2

It wasn't hard to get into Tuco's apartment. It used to be my garage before I converted it into an office and then finally his apartment. I know where Tuco hides the key. I tossed it pretty good.

Tacked to the wall I found an empty envelope, no name or return address, hotel stationery, stamp canceled in Milwaukee just a little more than a month ago. There were several books. A couple of old John Le Carre novels, some Robert B. Parker, and a small little volume that turned out to be a well worn hardback copy of Shakespeare's Henry V. Tuco's got a thing about Shakespeare. There wasn't a letter from the envelope in any of them.

There was something significant. Folded into Shakespeare was a printout of our El Tee's platoon roster.

Our old platoon commander has been obsessively scouring the Internet to find the guys in Recon. These were some forty odd names he'd found so far. Maybe Tuco called somebody. Maybe more than one somebody. Maybe I'd have to talk to the El Tee whether I wanted to or not.

Tuco had packed, but lightly, and casually. Wherever he was going he wasn't expecting to make a good impression. His two good dress shirts and his sports jacket were still hanging in the closet, nothing in the pockets. Both pairs of athletic shoes were gone and so were his boots.

Tuco's a bit of a gun nut. I had bought him a Kimber 1911 for the job, but he also had an AR-15, a Remington 700 deer rifle, a shotgun, and a stupid little Derringer. I couldn't find any, no guns, no ammo, and no cleaning kit. He wasn't just carrying; he'd packed the whole armory. There was plenty of room in his truck.

I pulled up the chair at his desk, an uncluttered workplace. His old laptop was plugged into power, but turned off, external mouse on mouse pad. There was a big porcelain cup painted with the Vietnam Service ribbon and stuffed full of pens and pencils.

Two pencils sat on a blank pad of paper, one crossed over the other. Tuco's a doodler, but there wasn't the slightest scrawl on the pad.

I held the pad edge on so I could view it from a low angle in the good light of the window. The only strong impressions I saw looked only as if he'd drawn with some force a big X through the whole page.

I tore off several top pages of the pad together, rolled them up and stuck them in my jacket pocket. I could buy a tube of graphite at any auto parts store and dust the page to get a better image.

Meanwhile I used the pad to take notes.

I turned on his old laptop. Since he didn't take it with him, he probably he only packed what he could carry in his trailer or on his bike. He was still running Microsoft XP without logon security. Nothing seemed password protected except for his email. By modern standards of computer paranoia, Tuco was a slacker.

I checked his email first. The oldest unread message was almost a month old. Lucky for me it was commercial spam, sending him the latest bargains available to Prize Club users on their premium website. There were three messages from them when I started and a fourth rolled in while I was reading the rest of Tuco's email.

The date on the spam, seemed to confirm he left a month ago, but there was a big gap between first date and the latest mail. Odd, I thought.

Most of the rest of the mail seemed to be stuff from a couple of Yahoo message groups. One of them was pretty active. I read far more than I cared to about a three wheeled motorcycle with a diesel engine that was supposed to change the world. One of the Recon guys wrote asking questions about some combat action long forgotten.

There were two personal emails that I paid some close attention to.

The first, a week old, was from somebody I knew, Al Starr, a pastor at a church in Lafayette and our group therapist. Tuco had missed group for more than a month. Don't think I didn't notice, wrote Pastor Al. I'm coming to get you if you don't show up again.

There was nothing further from Pastor Al, no follow up to the week old message though the group with me in it had met since. At a good guess Tuco and Al had talked. It might be tricky to find out about what. If Tuco consulted Al either as his shrink or spiritual advisor, Al could consider the conversation confidential.

I'd blush to quote too much from another email from one Yearning66. Tuco's email name is WarBear60. The salutation line was "Dearest Bear." She asked why he thought she wasn't trustworthy. She asked why he expected anyone could find her. She asked why he'd think she would tell anyone anything he'd asked her to keep secret. It was madness to leave and not tell her where he was going. She missed him terribly.

I didn't have too much chance to find Yearning by address. Certainly it can be done, but I don't know how. A guy would have to be a pretty heavy geek or have legal juice with the provider that I certainly couldn't get.

I might sweet talk Yearning. Maybe I could get her to tell me what she knew. It wouldn't be easy. I couldn't talk to her. I'd have to charm her in an email. I'd be trying to sweet talk a woman that I'd never seen with no better recommendation than my imagination and writing skills.

I printed her email just in case.

I poked around Tuco's computer for a bit, but he seemed to have erased tracks. There wasn't any more email. He deleted all of the earlier stuff. I wasn't shocked when I found his Internet History, Preferences, etc. were all cleared from Explorer. The "My Recent Documents" folder did have a shortcut to a document called Newton Report, but when I clicked on the shortcut, the document was gone.

I pulled open each of the drawers of the desk and glanced at the contents. There was nothing remarkable in them, pencils, pens, sketch pads, and junk – old pocket knives, spare change, random CD's, and half of a Mr. Goodbar.

Nothing seemed significant or appetizing.

An ordinary person who searched a friend's room in his own house might have stopped right there. I didn't. Maybe I'm retired but I still think like a cop.

In the desk there were two drawers to the left and three to the right. I started at the drawer on the bottom left, alternating sides. Without thinking too much about it, I ran my fingers in a quick sweep of the bottom of each of the drawers. This was a casual search of a friend's room. I'd no reason to expect him to hide anything there, but none the less my fingers swept the bottom of each drawer and found an envelope taped to the underside of the middle right drawer.

It wasn't sealed, just taped in place. On the outside of the envelope was written C237. There was a padlock key inside, a Schlage. I had several just like it. Maybe this was one of those. Maybe Tuco had borrowed my lock.

I rolled up the envelope around the key and jammed it in my wallet.

I pushed the chair back, settled myself in it, and put my feet up on the desk with the pad paper and both pencils in hand.

Tuco had been gone a month, and he wasn't expecting to dress up nice when he got where he was going. He was carrying his weapons and all of his ammo. Maybe he was scared badly of something or maybe he just wanted the guns for comfort. Sometimes when Tuco gets agitated he takes his guns and heads for the woods, but scared is agitated too. Not really a shock if somehow he was connected to Newton and had learned of his death.

Maybe Al Starr knew something about what Tuco was doing, because Al wasn't asking about it anymore.

Maybe the letter was from one of our old buddies. He'd printed the El Tee's phone list. The El Tee was always writing to us keeping up our connection. Maybe the El Tee could put something out about Tuco and make some calls.

New thought. Wherever Tuco was he didn't have easy access to the Internet. He'd left his laptop. He'd still want access sometimes if he had a romance going with Yearning. Probably he was using a public terminal, maybe at a library, using webmail. There was enough mail here I didn't think he visited the library that often, but surely more often than some of this old spam. Maybe he'd never deleted it. Maybe on purpose.

When you read email with Outlook, the messages are automatically deleted from the server. With webmail you have to manually delete each.

Next time Tuco went to the public library for his mail he could see the spam was gone. He might even have left it there as a tell, like super spy leaves a hair across the crack of a door. If he thought about it, he would know I'd been here or someone had because the spam would be gone.

Schooner was probably right. Tuco was somehow tangled up with Glowery in the Newton murder. Why else delete the Newton report file. Even without the report I could trace his progress because I knew the starting point, our client.

I ought to think about ways to get to know Yearning. She sounded trustworthy to me, and probably to him. He was trying to bury himself plenty deep if he wouldn't tell her where he was going.

I now felt certain Tuco was in some kind of trouble, but he didn't want me involved. I couldn't think of any other reason for him to clean out his email. He didn't want any tracks left behind that anyone could follow, even me, unless you counted the key.

I found myself smiling. Maybe Tuco left me another kind of message.

Long ago in the Non Commissioned Officers Candidate School at Ft. Benning, they taught us small unit tactics using doctrines that began with Roger's Rangers. Our particular instructor spoke of the Ranger's traditional trail signs.

Crossed sticks on a trail do not fall that way naturally. The trailblazer crosses them to warn those behind not to follow.

I pulled out the rolled sample I'd torn from the pad, held it to the light and sideways to look at the indentations. Tuco had marked an X on the paper, but torn off that page, maybe to use it for something else. Maybe the X wasn't meant as a warning, or maybe he wasn't sure and kept changing his mind. I'd found the pad with two crossed sticks, in this case pencils.

Maybe Tuco simply tossed the pencils at the desk and they fell one leaning on the other. Maybe anything random or accidental, or....maybe he had tried to leave me a message.

Maybe not.

Our minds make patterns and assign them meaning, real or not.

If Tuco left no message, he had left me in the dark. But it don't mean nothing. I would follow.

I walked around the apartment and took some time straightening up. If Tuco had been gone a month he wasn't likely to notice anything not too badly out of place.

I grabbed the door knob to let myself out when a gunshot rang out.

"Stay in that apartment, you thieving bastard," she said. "I've got a gun and know how to use it, and cops are on the way."

"Lily, don't shoot," I called. "It's just me your ever loving husband."

CHAPTER 3

"My God," she said. "I ... could have killed you."

I opened the door and stepped out. She was crying, shaking, and still holding her Ladysmith pointed at the ground. I took her gun hand gently, asked her to let go, and then gathered her in my arms.

"You've threatened a time or two," I said quietly.

Lily's quite good with her gun. I've made her practice, not only with target shooting but also some combat simulations. Maybe she'd never before quite owned up to the possibility of actually shooting somebody, and certainly not the somebody who had been her lover for more than thirty years.

"Take it easy," I said. "Why don't you just step into Tuco's place and sit down."

"We... We should be outside," she gasped. "I called Vinson."

She was right. Mark Vinson was my driver and partner on the El Sobrante force before I retired. Lily had reported an intruder. If he couldn't easily find her, he might assume the worst. Safer for us to wait outside.

Lily dabbed at her eyes with a tissue. "I must look a mess."

"You're fine," I said. "You're always fine."

"I was an idiot."

"No," I said. "This is my fault. I shouldn't have come without telling you first. I just didn't think of it. You're supposed to be at work."

She glared at me. "That means you did think of it. You thought you could get this done and never tell me."

"Well yeah. What would be the point?"

"What is the point?"

"Tuco may be in trouble" I said. "He was on a case. He was after a missing guy who turned up dead. Schooner thinks Glowery is behind it. I thought I'd look around."

"That's why Bob called me the other day asking for Tuco?"

"Yeah," I said. "When you said you hadn't seen Tuco for a month he thought I should know about it."

"Is he in trouble?" She asked.

"Yeah," I said slowly. "I think so."

Vinson pulled a squad car into the driveway. Tuco's apartment is a garage conversion behind my house. We never took the driveway out.

Vinson stepped out of the car and pulled off his sunglasses.

"Trouble?" He asked.

"Just me," I said. "I was in Tuco's apartment but didn't tell her I was coming."

"Sorry Mark," Lily said. "I guess I'm a little jumpy."

Vinson shrugged. "Maybe I would be too."

She smiled ruefully.

I'm a detective; I thought I detected something.

"What happened?" I asked.

"The burglar alarm went off last week," Lily said

"Were you here? Did they get anything? Why didn't you call me?"

"Calm down. That's why I didn't call you.

"There was never any reason to worry. I was already in bed. I got the phone and my Ladysmith, opened the door to the bedroom, and sat in my big chair. I was practically invisible. Anybody at the doorway would make a nice silhouette target back lit from the street. I called 911. The patrol car was here in less than two minutes."

"Probably some damn druggie," I said. "The saddest neighborhood in Richmond is only about four miles west of here. A real thief would know better than to break into even an ex-Police Chief's house! Did they catch anybody?"

"No. They drove around that night and didn't see anybody."

"The guy probably wasn't on the street."

I didn't explain. I didn't have to for Lily. A trail head for the Wildcat Canyon Park is only three blocks from our house. The Park District maintains several parks in Alameda and Contra Costa Counties. The trails in most cases were also fire roads. If the Chief asked for helicopters he could have checked them. I'd have done it. This Chief would not; an unsuccessful break in was hardly worth the cost.

"Also," Lily said, "it turns out they weren't trying to break into the house. They were trying to break into Tuco's room."

"It's still my damned house!"

"Yes but why would some poor drugged soul go after the garage?"

"He might have been after cars or contents."

"Well... maybe not," Vinson said. "I came around the next morning. Since you've converted this garage, Lily's car was here in the driveway and it wasn't locked.

"You know I keep change for bridge fare," Lily said. "It was still there in the ashtray where I left it."

A happy addict would have grabbed that in a second.

"I noticed Tuco's guns were gone. Was it burglary?"

"The guns were gone before the break in," Lily said. "I had a look around when I discovered Tuco had gone."

"What do you guys think?" I asked Vinson.

He shrugged. "Maybe a test run. Maybe just a look around. Maybe he hoped to find Tuco, but found the alarm instead."

Maybe.

"Thanks for coming, Mark. Sorry we wasted your time."

He smiled. "On a good day they're all false alarms."

CHAPTER 4

"Were you going to talk to me?"

"Guess I've got to," I said. "As far as I know you're the last person to see Tuco."

"But you were going to put it off."

"Because I knew you'd give me a load of crap," I said.

"Stay for dinner," she said.

Maybe I was 60 years old, but sometimes she still makes me feel like I'm 15 on my first date.

She led me into the house, shut the door turned and kissed me.

It's not magic. When you love someone a long time, each of you learns how to move with the other, each knows best where to find ease and comfort. Lily always rests her right cheek on my left shoulder, and I find I always turn my cheek against the top of her head. We are, for most of the world, old folks now, but she still looks good to me.

At five foot eleven, she is only three inches shy of my own height. She weighs more than she thinks any woman should admit. On a frame so tall the number is meaningless. I think she's too skinny. She spends way too much time on her treadmill or at the gym.

We've grown old together. Her hair's white; I tease I've always wanted a platinum blond. Her face is a map of her life, lined now, but not yet as deeply lined as it will be. Her cheekbones will always be high, her mouth at rest unsmiling but for me always surmounted by her lovely, penetrating green eyes. She's embarrassed now by her neck and wears scarves.

Lily was born in Boston, Irish, not Brahman, but patrician enough for me. She got a scholarship to Sarah Lawrence, but dropped out after she spent the summer of '66 in Mississippi where, for protest, she arrived married to Karen's birth father, black skinned Owen Albright.

He was a handsome man. I've seen pictures. She loved him in her fashion, she says, though they did not live much together after '67. He was drafted in '67 and died in the Tet Offensive in '68 without ever seeing Karen.

I met Lily visiting Tuco at Letterman Army Hospital. The tall aloof blond visiting wounded veterans, though family to none, intrigued me, attracted me.

She was happy to share a cup of coffee, but for a long time would not share more. When she brought Karen to Letterman, I knew why she didn't seem to have time for me at night. I knew I was a goner. I was smitten, not only with Lily but also Karen. Tuco approved, and teased me about it.

"She was there for me, bro, me not you, me the wounded Apache/Chicano brother, not you the untouched paleface. She's too good for you, and you've got to be a better poppa than I see now."

He was vastly amused by his own joke. We all knew Tuco was neither Chicano nor Apache, just another Filipino who passed.

I invited Karen along with Lily on our first date. I don't remember what the movie was but I know it was for kids. I spent most of the time whispering to Karen while holding Lily's hand. I got immediate feedback from her hand. I think on that first night I qualified as a father if not husband.

Kissing her is still an adventure after 35 years.

And her cooking's great. Mine's not bad she says, and she thinks my larger hands make me a better bread maker than she is. I can't tell the difference. I wasn't baking bread at Floyd's place in El Cerrito and I was glad to have hers in El Sobrante.

"No talk of Tuco until after dinner," she decreed.

That wasn't hard.

She'd uncorked a favorite wine, Old Vine Zin, a tasty wine and a memory of the day we bought it.

I'm still fool enough to try for repeats of magic days.

"Here's looking at you, kid. Let's go back one day and get some more of this."

She didn't miss a beat.

"So when are you moving back?"

She's always spoiling for this fight. As I get older, I have become more direct. Around Lily right now it's as if we're naked when we're dressed.

"Just as soon as I know you're safe."

She grimaced. "I take my own risks. You're not responsible for my safety."

"But I am responsible for my actions."

"When you're asleep, Duvall? For Christ sake."

"Christ's got nothing to do with it.

"It was a real bummer of a dream. My hands were really around your throat. I might have killed you. I'd have to forgive myself. I'm responsible until I'm dead... and some say always."

Her eyes smiled, but with tears, and the smile wasn't on her mouth.

"Only if I don't kill you first while you're awake."

I had tears of my own, but I smiled through them. "Cut the crap, toughie. You're just being cross because I haven't taken you to bed."

She stood up, held out her hand, and in a dark, rough voice said, "Do that now."

We postponed all talk of Tuco until the morning. Before I could fall asleep I kissed her again and got up.

"I'll be in Tuco's bed."

"It will be lonely," she said. "Maybe you forgot? He isn't there."

"It would still be lonely if he was. It's never him I want

to sleep with."

"You could sleep here, but you won't do it."

"I can't."

An eyebrow arched over her smile. Now she was in a far better humor, saucy instead of angry.

"You choose not to."

"I do choose. I must."

She opened the drawer of her nightstand and took out an ashtray and a pack of Virginia Slims. She was smoking again. I might have noticed the faint, masked smell but I was too distracted to pay attention.

"Don't be cross. I know about must," she said. "This is just an oral substitute."

She sat cross legged on the bed naked without the signature scarf. The blue veins prominent in her skin makes it seem fluorescent white. She sags now where once she was elastic. Her body is haunted by lines, moles, and unexpected hairs, but she owns it completely, a possession well used for all of its purpose, gorgeously inhabited by her 64 years.

"Cigarettes are bad for you."

"Less bad when you're old. Less to lose. How soon can you move back and make me quit?"

"I don't make you do anything. I just show up to see what you do."

"Like the show?"

"Your biggest fan."

"So stick around. I've got interesting bumps. Maybe it's going to be a bumpy night."

"Thanks, but no thanks. It won't be. I'm an old man too. I'm going to sleep."

She grabbed my right hand in both of hers. Her eyes welled not quite to tears. "Please, George. When are we going to fix this?"

"I'm fixing it now. I'm just not finished. I do more therapy, you know, usually three hours a week."

"It's really worse since you started with that group."

"If some thing's bad wrong with Tuco, I may end up doing more. It could get worse."

I had a bad night.

In the morning I found Tuco's spare razor and a toothbrush still in cellophane. I've never known him to bring a woman home in all the years he's lived here, but he was prepared. I shaved, brushed my teeth and stood a long time under the hot water in Tuco's shower, before I dressed and went to the house.

"Bacon and eggs?" she asked.

"Yes, thank you. Coffee?"

She handed me an over sized mug. With a little milk the coffee was hot and rich.

I pulled out a stool at the island in the kitchen. "So talk about Tuco."

The bacon began to sizzle in her mother's cast iron skillet. She wiped her hands on her apron, and sipped black coffee from her cup.

"He'd been traveling. One of your cases. He got back four or five weeks ago."

"Interesting. I haven't seen a report, not even one, and he's been gone six weeks. I haven't seen him. I haven't paid him."

"A letter came for him while he was gone. I watched him open it. He..."

"Go on," I said. "I think I saw the envelope."

"Well he didn't look right. You know how expressive he can be. He didn't change color or anything like that, but he'd been smiling, chatting away, and now I was looking at his poker face.

"I asked him if there was anything wrong. He said no, and stuffed the envelope and letter in his jacket pocket. That's when it started."

Tuco doesn't have credit cards, doesn't borrow money, and has only a cell phone. "No strings on me," he says. He doesn't get much mail. When he does it's personal. In the absence of another address it all comes to us.

This time he'd been gone for more than a month and there was nothing new.

"Tell me about the letter," I said, "I think maybe I saw the envelope. He's got that tacked to the wall over his desk."

"I don't know anything. You saw the envelope. No return address but I noticed it was from Milwaukee. I don't know anybody in Milwaukee."

"Could be the El Tee," I said, "but that wouldn't shake him much and this did?"

"Uh huh. I noticed he was spending more time with me. He seemed to want to talk, but he wasn't saying anything. Well, you know... something. He told me all of your old war stories again. By now I've heard them all in two versions about a thousand times."

"Apparently he needed to tell them."

Usually Tuco doesn't talk much about the war except to me or the group. Lily's really only heard a few war stories from him. She thinks there are many stories because she squirms watching what Tuco goes through to tell them.

"So you think what's going on is about the war?" I asked.

"I'm sure of it. He told me a veteran friend got killed. He said the guy was probably his best friend in the world but for you and me. He said he'd thought his friend was strong, but now he knew the man just knew how to mask being weak."

Maybe he was worried about how strong he was himself. I knew the burden he carried. Lily did not. The dead friend had to be Newton.

She turned the bacon with a fork.

"Anything else?"

She wiped her hands on the apron again and grabbed mine. I have larger hands, but she grabbed as much as she could.

"I noticed he was cleaning his guns almost every day."

Lily knows me and she knows Tuco. She's lived a lifetime with me and close to him.

Tuco has a permit for his handgun. He got the permit as my operative, and it was wise to carry if we were doing something nuts like chasing bail jumpers. Tuco didn't have a permit before he worked for me, but he's always had his guns around. He only carried the pistol when he had a reason. Sometimes that reason was just because it made him feel better.

She squeezed my hands, and I squeezed back.

"And?"

She drained the bacon on a plate covered with paper towels. The eggs were next.

"And nothing I can point to. I just knew there was something wrong, something nagging him. He'd probably been gone a couple of days before I noticed. At first I just thought he'd gotten over the problem, and then I noticed the light in there was on all the time."

She always breaks her eggs one handed. Each gets a sharp rap on the edge of the skillet, and somehow she pulls the shell apart one-handed. I watched her for a long time. She's shown me how. I can never do it, and her yolks never crack.

She wiped her hands on a dish towel and turned to face me. She had something to say that she thought was important.

"The real thing is he didn't say goodbye. Until now he always did. I think for him it's part of being polite. He lives in my house, and he always made sure I knew whether to expect him here or not."

I pulled out my cell phone. "Did you call him?"

"Of course I called. I wasn't going to worry if I could find out where he was. Every call I made went straight to voice mail. Now I only get a busy signal."

"His voice mail box must be full. Maybe he's turned off his phone. Maybe he's out of range," I said.

She folded her arms, and grabbed each elbow with the opposite hand and shuddered a little. "I hope so," she said. "From what you've told me about Glowery, he should get as far away as he can."

"Not too far," I said. "He could probably use my help."

We talked a bit more, but really just for the pleasure of our company. There was nothing more about Tuco that she could tell me.

We kissed and I held her a long time before I left.

"Find our friend," she said.

CHAPTER 5

Al Starr said he had a quiet day. He could see me that afternoon at three.

"Come to the house," he said and gave me directions.

Al lives in Martinez.

I took the back way out on Pinole Valley Road, mostly two lanes, but sometimes one, a back road lots more fun in my Z3 than Highway 4.

I found Al's place near the Courthouse in an old neighborhood where no one has a garage and the street isn't really wide enough to drive because of all the cars in the street.

I eased the Z3 up onto a root tumbled sidewalk to leave enough road for other cars to pass. Old Martinez wasn't really designed for cars.

Al appeared in the doorway, a California Buddha. He wore sandals and shorts for the heat and tented his big belly under a cotton Hawaiian shirt, formerly a bright red, now faded to a red pink.

"Come in, George," he said at the door. "I get to work at home because my wife's away on a trip with her sister. We can talk inside or out here on the porch."

The house was a little Arts and Crafts bungalow with a tiny front yard. The porch crossed the whole width of the house, effectively another room, a place you could sit to greet your neighbors on the street.

Martinez sits between the San Joaquin River and San Pablo Bay before it widens and becomes San Francisco Bay. Where Al lives it still feels like a small town, but it certainly isn't anymore. There's a major oil refinery there and two freeways, one bisecting Martinez, the other just to the East through Pacheco.

I like small towns, but this one, like most on the east side of the hills, is too warm for me, a good ten degrees hotter than El Sobrante or Pinole. I chose the shaded porch and hoped for breeze.

"Something to drink?" Al asked.

"Iced tea?"

Al grinned. "Suit yourself. You said this wasn't therapy. I'm having beer. I've got a six pack of Fat Tire cold." He slapped his ample belly. "Built by Al one beer at a time!"

"Beer's good."

"It's lovely on a hot day, but I'm not supposed drink during therapy. If this isn't therapy it must be spiritual guidance."

Al brought out a couple of tall glasses. He put them on a wrought iron table topped with glass between two bent cane rockers. He went back into the house and rummaged about in a distant kitchen. I heard the distant rattle of ice. He returned with a Rubbermaid bucket full of bottled beer and ice. He put the bucket down on the table with the glasses. We sat in the rockers. He took an opener from the bucket and popped the caps on two cold ones, pouring each in a glass.

"Glad you called, George. I've hoped to get some time with you alone. I've thought you haven't got quite so much out of group as others do."

"I'm not exactly here for me. It's more for Tuco."

He nodded. "Tuco."

He spilled a little beer on the porch. "That's the sacrifice. Now let me sanctify this with prayer."

It's always the same prayer. It doesn't sound hokey because he means it.

"Lord we meet as comrades, your warriors seeking truth and comfort. Lord please send us your holy spirit and grant us the grace we earned as your brothers in blood.

"To absent friends."

"Crispin Crispian," I said.

I'll always drink to that, and so will Al. He's a lot of man, a trained therapist, an ordained minister, and a Vietnam combat vet, same outfit as my friend Floyd, the 1st of the 9th Marines, The Walking Dead. He's sure not dead, in fact more alive than most. I'll always feel lucky to have found him.

"My oh, my," he said, putting down a much shorter beer, "Another great day in America. Now tell me what's so special about you and Tuco?"

"Nothing very special. We were in the same outfit, in fact the same platoon. Pretty much I was with him or he was with me for most of our war. He got hit and ended up at Letterman. When I got out, I came to see him."

"Let's pretend I'm a civilian," said Al. "Why did you do that?"

"He was my partner. He got hurt. When I got home I went to see him."

"Sure. I know. You just said that. And why?"

"He was my partner."

Al took a long pull on his beer.

"George, for Vietnam, that's not an answer. Most of us came home and never saw those guys again. I know there are recent exceptions. We're becoming old men. It's time to make sense of what we did when young. Some of us are finding ourselves and some of us are finding each other."

"I guess that's what group is for."

"For some, but please don't change the subject. You came home. You found your buddy. As far as I can tell you've been more or less glued together ever since."

"Not quite. He took a ten year vacation first. Anyway he is my oldest and best friend."

"You're more different than you're alike."

I took a pull on my own beer. I could guess where he was going with this and I wished he wasn't. Al was just doing his job as he saw it, but that wasn't going to be easy on me. I wasn't going to tell him about the old woman, so I tried a diversion.

"I came about Tuco, Al. He's disappeared." In a few minutes I gave him the bare bones of it, Newton dead with Tuco gone, packing heat, and according to my wife more than a little upset.

"About what exactly?"

"She thinks about the war. He's been telling too many stories."

"So Tuco's gone walkabout," Al said.

"Yeah."

"How old is Tuco?"

"Fifty seven," I said."

"Is he married?"

"No. I think you know he isn't."

"Does he owe you money?"

"No."

"He's not working right now, not for you or anyone you know of?

"I guess not. He seems to have finished his last work for me though I haven't seen a report."

"So who appointed you to be his nanny? He seems to have no obligations outstanding, no commitments we know about, and nothing to stop him from roaming about the country any way he likes - a free citizen. I'll chew him out for missing group when he gets back and that will be that."

"I told you about the dead guy, the gun, and ammo."

"So you did. So what? He's permitted, you said. He's legally allowed to walk around with a concealed piece. Maybe he intends on going someplace dangerous. Maybe he'll try to take a vacation in good old Vietnam. What business is it of yours, Duvall?"

If he was trying to get me mad, he was beginning to succeed.

"Chill, Al. You know the score. Tuco and I went through everything. We were in bad spots and fought our way out. He watched my back, and I watched his. You know what that means. You were there. You know it wasn't always pretty, but he has always watched my back, and I will always watch his."

"I do know. I was there."

"If he's in a jam it's my job to get him out. He'd do the same for me."

"Really?" said Al. "I know there's a war on now, but it isn't yours. You guys are done. You finished fighting yours at least 31 years ago today."

I took a deep breath and let it out slowly. "Maybe not," I said. "Maybe some of the fight never stops. I thought I got home a long time ago, but maybe I just didn't quite make it."

We sat for a minute listening to lawn sprinklers, sipping beer. We caught a bit of breeze coming up the channel.

"You don't talk much in group."

"I told you. I'm not there for me. I don't have so much of a problem."

"Right," said Al. "I forgot your life was so normal. Let's look at a few points. You admit to getting the jumps. You've moved out of your house because you're afraid you'll kill your wife in your sleep. When someone worries about your friend, you decide he has taken off, and it maybe has something to do with the war, but you don't have a problem."

"Let's get this under control, Al. I know I twitch, but most of the time I ignore it. I'll try to talk more. I'll tell you what I can. I do want some help. It'd be nice to move back into my own house."

"Tuco doesn't talk much either."

"When I find him you can ask him if he can be talkative. Do you know where he is?"

"Sorry, Duvall. I have no clue to give you. He's said nothing to me about where he might hide."

"You could let me decide that. You could tell me what he said."

"No I couldn't. He told me in confidence, and I must respect that, spiritually and professionally. He did come to see me, but there's nothing I can say about that now."

"He could be in real trouble, Al. I mean the spiritual kind. He can get down on himself pretty bad. Sometimes that old war is too much to handle."

Al swiveled his rocker in my direction and took a long pull on his beer. "Do you know something specific?"

Time to remind him about the toddler at the gate. Tuco had already told it in group. The tale haunts most people. If I didn't know there was worse, it might haunt me. Maybe if it moved Al he'd tell me more if he could.

"Remember the story of how Tuco killed that kid?"

Al nodded and opened another beer. Once again he spilled a little on the porch. "That's not it, George. That'd bother some people. Maybe it sometimes bothers Tuco, but it's not the worst thing." He wiped the iced down bottle of beer across the perspiration on his forehead.

"That's only a story about him. That's not what you and he have trouble living with."

It sure was getting hot. I was sweating too, a little dizzy, and a bit off balance.

Maybe I knew the trouble Al was talking about even if he didn't.

Al sat quietly, beer in hand, but not drinking, just watching me.

I felt I had to talk. "I don't know if you know, Al. I was there in Vietnam when Tuco got hit. In fact I was walking point. It was a chicom claymore. I walked right past it. Everybody got fucked up but me and the kid walking drag. I'm entitled to my survivor guilt, and I'm guilty about Tuco."

He closed his eyes. His mouth made funny motions before he spoke. "That's not it either."

"What makes you think so?" I asked.

"My job, George. I'm supposed to listen. When you're here, you get all my attention. I pray too. Eventually the patterns are clear.

"When you or Tuco talk, it's like watching an old married couple. Even now. You're looking for Tuco just as you'd look for a wife. You can't really imagine Tuco going missing, and if he had to leave, you were sure he'd tell you why, but he didn't.

"In group when either one of you talk you always speak with caution and consent. Each of you watches the other...still. You've still got his back, and he's still got yours.

"Go ahead, Duvall. Tell me it isn't true."

"Lots of what you say is true, Al. I've watched his backside most of my life, and he's watched mine. I met my wife visiting him at Letterman. Our lives have always been knit together, though we are very different people. I trust him more than I can yet trust you, and I'm sure he feels the same."

"Sure," said Al. "He's got to. So do you. You have to trust each other to not talk about it – whatever it is."

I decided to come clean a little. "You're right. There is a story. I don't tell it because it's Tuco's story, not mine. I was there, but only a witness except I didn't really see anything. Tuco can tell you if he wants to, but I can't. That's why I worry. Sometimes Tuco says he feels as if there's a spring inside him all wound up, but he doesn't know where or when it will unwind or what it will do."

"There's a spring in you too, Duvall. You don't trust it either."

"But I can watch out for him, and maybe he can watch out for me."

"And maybe neither of you can. A man's soul is his own, Duvall. You can't save anybody who isn't willing to be saved."

"I can do without the soul stuff, Al. It's either truth or bullshit. I can't tell. If I can't tell, it don't mean nothing."

Al put his hand on my shoulder. "I just mean it's not your job to fix what Tuco feels. Each of you can only be responsible for yourself."

I brushed his hand off my shoulder. "And how's that? What's the magic formula? I feel awful because I know my friend's in trouble."

"That's a feeling I know pretty well," he said. "I have many friends in trouble. One of them is you. Tuco's another."

Al drained his glass. "Spiritual counseling is always thirsty work. Everybody's got to believe in something. I believe you'll have another beer."

Bathed for many minutes in the bucket of ice, my second Fat Tire was far colder than the first. I didn't bother with the glass. The cold bottle was pleasant in my hands and against my forearms in the heat.

"Some of us got out of the war with fewer scars than others," Al said. "I've found most of the guys in my old unit. Most are fine. Some are better than fine. Some are a mess and some are dead. Between the fine ones and the messes you'd never think there'd be much difference. It's a mystery to me."

"Me too," I said.

"I've read all the literature," Al said. "There are theories. There's effective clinical practice. I do the best I can. I do all right. I can't help everyone, but I do help some. Even when I do help, I often don't know what I did.

"I can't promise you guys anything. I don't know anything. I do have my guesses. And about Tuco, I do have a guess."

"Yes?"

"I can see how strong the bond is between you. You're still watching his back, and surely he's still watching yours. What you need to ask is: What's he doing to watch your back right now?"

I paused.

Pencil X's on paper. Tuco had warned me.

I am a trained investigator. I look at records and people, and see patterns. I accumulate facts and compare them one to another. I develop theories and test the results. I can assemble a fact pattern that may usefully be used in court. I am infinitely objective. I have no hidden agendas. For most of my life it has been my work to find facts and show them in the light.

None of this helped me now.

I don't know everything about Tuco, but he is my oldest friend. I know the generosity of his heart and the weakness of his hair trigger temper, but his life isn't simple, and I don't live it for him.

Al proposed a new fact pattern. I knew I took care of Tuco, but maybe I never quite recognized how he took care of me.

Did it matter? I was less sure than Al. But it was a theory I could examine.

"Come and see me when you're ready to talk," Al said. "Sometimes the only way out is through."

CHAPTER 6

I drank coffee with Floyd Robbins on Monday morning, while he ate breakfast. Floyd's house is in El Cerrito. I don't impinge on his privacy too much. He's rented me his cottage in the back.

"So what's your next step?" he asked, when I told him about Tuco.

"Lily didn't know she could file a missing person's report. I think I'll go down to my old station and do that. I've got a picture I can give them."

Floyd looked a little bemused. "I thought the cops were already looking for him?"

"Not really. They're leaving that to me. A missing person report should get him broader coverage. In California, they have to take the report. That doesn't mean they have to work it very hard, but I hope the guys who worked for me will at least keep an eye out."

"Yeah sure," Floyd said.

"Take a little on faith, Floyd."

I could've phoned in a report. I could've submitted it over the Internet to a web page. I chose to drive in and make a face to face report. Perhaps that wasn't wise.

The station is on the northwest side of Appian Way near the intersection with Valley View. It's a modest building, two stories and a flat roof and an overused antenna mast, too much like so many other civic structures, block like, but unimposing. El Sobrante does not have a large police force, but it's big enough.

I parked in a slot marked visitor. I'd heard the new Chief was a stickler about the parking slots. Bob Haas was the desk sergeant today. I still thought of him as a young athletic patrolman, but now he's losing his hair and waistline.

"How are you doing, Chief. Business or pleasure."

"Business, Bob. Wish it wasn't. A missing person's report."

"Young one?"

The rules that mandate missing person reports in California were written largely for children.

"Fortunately not. Male adult about my age." Just routine, in another words.

"Well let's see who's up...."

"Hey George."

Vinson grabbed my hand and gave me a bear hug. He was my driver and staff guy for my last nine years. He's only a few years younger than I, but still in great shape, certainly better than Bob. I was a little surprised he was working the bullpen.

"Let me take this, Bob."

Haas said, "Yeah." I followed Vinny back to his cube.

"You been good, Chief?"

"Pretty much," I told him, "but I get the yips lately."

"Not a surprise."

Vinny was just young enough that he missed the Vietnam draft. His brothers got caught so he didn't laugh at those of us who had to go.

"So what can I do for you now?"

"You remember Tuco."

"Sure. I've been hearing some things."

"He's gone missing."

"Suspiciously?"

"Not so much you guys will notice except a body turned up."

"Why don't you give that to me straight?"

"Okay. A guy Tuco was looking for has turned up dead. Tuco's been gone about two weeks. He didn't tell anybody he was going. He took his whole gun kit with him; he's licensed as my operative. I thought he was working a missing person case, the dead guy, but he seemed to have finished it because he was home four weeks ago. Lily says he's been agitated and talking a lot about Vietnam ever since he got a letter."

"And there was an attempted break in the other night on his room," Vinson said. "I'll take a report."

"Of course you will. This is California."

"Last time I checked."

"So what's Tuco's full name."

"Jorge Jesus Luis Ruis."

"Lotta names, A.K.A. Tuco the Rat."

"That's the way they did it in his folks' country. Lots of names. Want to know something funny? Tuco means tomato sauce in Spanish. It doesn't mean rat. Maybe it's rat in Italian."

"Really?"

"Tuco looked it up on the Internet."

Vinnie looked up from his form. "How'd he get the Tuco handle anyway?"

"I am George and he is Jorge. That was a bit confusing for the grunts we were running with. I was tall, skinny, and blond and suppose I could vaguely be said to resemble Eastwood. Jorge was a short latin looking. Someone called us Blondie and Tuco and Tuco said, 'I know this movie!'

"By the time I left Vietnam I doubt there was a grunt in Recon who knew my name. I was Blondie, Sgt. Blondie on formal occasions, and Tuco's been Tuco ever since."

"You got SS numbers or anything?"

I handed him the personnel file I keep on Tuco for my business. Bob ran through his form matching fields from mine. "There are no credit cards," I told him, "Tuco doesn't believe in them. He thinks they are a way that somebody could find him."

"He'd be right. What about health insurance?"

"That's why he's cheap labor for me. I don't have to pay it. He goes to VA. Tuco's not exactly a willing participant in modern society, except for his cell phone."

"Who is?" Vinnie asked, as he furiously keyboarded a report. "I'd guess that you're looking into this yourself? What's your phone number these days, Chief?"

"I'm looking" I said. I followed the menus and gave him the number of my cell.

"Anything on my housebreaker?" I asked.

"Nothing much to speak of. Your prints. Lily's prints. Tuco's. Some guy with gloves. You know we'll do what we can," Vinnie said.

"Just as we would for any good taxpaying citizen," Chief Dornacker announced. He spoke just loudly enough to make sure the whole room could hear him. His head was just a couple of feet above mine, his chin cupped in his hands, elbows leaning on a partition wall of the cubicle.

"What's his beef, Vinson?"

"Missing person's report, Chief. And I updated him on his break in."

"Child?"

"No," I said, wanting the heat off Vinny, "a friend."

The Chief's right hand dropped slowly to the top of the partition. His left hand stroked his chin. His left eyebrow arched in a mockery of puzzlement. He looked down at me through bemused, half lidded eyes.

"I don't believe we have a priority for friends."

Dornacker sure wasn't one of mine. I don't know how the council picked him. I'd consulted with them during their search for a new Chief. I'd recommended someone else against him, and I was quite sure he knew that. When I was feeling paranoid, I felt sure Dornacker knew someone on the council better than he advertised.

"Of course not," I said. "Any fool could see that. I don't imagine a modern day police department can place much stock in friendship. I am merely making a report like any concerned citizen."

I'd have been better off phoning it in. Dornacker would never have noticed.

"Is it a complete report, Vinson?"

"Yes sir. We have everything we need."

"Probably more than enough," Dornacker said. "Let me assure you, Citizen Duvall. You'll get every consideration any other taxpayer does. We'll give you just exactly as much effort as we would for any man."

And no more, I was quite certain.

"Vinson, I'd better not find out you jumped the line to take this report from, Duvall."

"He was up, Chief," Haas called from the front desk.

"I'm sure that's what it will say in your record," Dornacker called back. "People listen up." Vinnie and two other folks in the cubes stood up.

"A modern police department is only as good as its discipline and procedures. These have been established for your benefit, and maximum efficiency. Follow them or expect to be caught not following them. Once you slip up..." Here he paused to glance first at Vinnie and then at Haas. "I'll be on your case."

"Don't stick your neck out for me, Vinnie," I said quietly.

"He can't chop it," Vinnie said. "I've been looking for another job, and I'll get one too. It's all CalPers retirement. Heck I'll probably get a better job. Too bad about the department though."

I picked up my file, and followed Dornacker into his office. Maybe that wasn't the smartest thing I should do, but I usually feel loathing if not fear for irrational authority.

"Chief I want to thank you for your personal consideration." I was being sarcastic and he knew it.

"Just doing my job, Mr. Duvall. Just doing my job." His grin was too broad, his tongue practically hanging out.

"Like you said. Your job. I'm retired from it. I don't want it anymore. Your department. Your business if you drive off good cops like Haas and Vinson. Don't worry. It won't hurt them. I can get them both better jobs in about ten minutes.

"It won't hurt them, but it will hurt you and your department, and it will hurt you politically. This town is too small. I'll bet there isn't a man on the city council who doesn't know them. Think about it."

I left. By now Floyd was off on one expedition or another. I drove down the hill to Dam Road and drove west. El Soleil is a great little cafe on the south side of Dam Road. Time for lunch. Over a french dip sandwich with potato salad, I thought about my next moves and drank coffee.

One step at a time; there were only two things I could think to do. I could graphite the paper I'd lifted from Tuco's room, and I could look over the files on the Newton case.

I finished my coffee and left some cash to pay for the meal and tip for the waitress. I took San Pablo instead of the freeway and found an Auto Zone where I bought a tube of graphite before heading for my lonely cottage.

CHAPTER 7

Floyd was still out and about.

I took the pad of paper from my jacket pocket and flattened it. A dusting with graphite brought out the big X across the page. Lower left to upper right of the X put a line through a name he'd written obliquely: Henry Newton. He'd also scrawled a phone number with a 707 prefix. Also the initials T.G. with a question mark.

The T.G. didn't mean anything to me right away, but of course anything to do with the Newton case was suggestive. Tuco was personally involved. I pored over my notes

My working case files were all pretty thin. On Newton I had a contract, client name, Theresa Garcia, the phone number, which matched, and a description of the problem, including several more details.

There was a mishmash of notes from Tuco about Newton, something of a crazy life. One of the notes mentioned Newton's father was a General. His parents were renowned and successful, but by Newton's own measure he was not. His marriage failed after his son committed suicide. Newton became self destructive, drugs and rehab. Our client met him at the drug rehab center. She worked there, but she seemed to be acting (in Tuco's opinion) like some kind of ex-girlfriend.

My file had my original contract, but not a copy of the email with the scan of Ms. Garcia's signature. Maybe I'd tossed it. What I had here was a copy of the one she had mailed. Maybe the email was already out to storage.

Nothing else here, there shouldn't be anything else out in storage either. I knew I didn't have a report yet. I couldn't think of anything else I wanted for the file.

Nothing for it; I dialed the phone.

"Teri Garcia speaking."

"Ms. Garcia, my name is George Duvall. Duvall Inquiry is the name of my business. I'm looking here at a contract with me that you signed on April 3."

"Yes, that was me, Mr. Duvall. What can I do for you?"

"I'm afraid the question is more, what did we do for you Ms. Garcia. You might think of this as a follow up call. Are you satisfied with our service?"

"Yes. Mr. Ruis did find my friend."

"So things worked out?"

"Much as I expected, but not quite as I hoped."

"Sorry if you're disappointed," I said. "Do you think we fulfilled our contract satisfactorily?"

"You did."

"I'm pleased to hear that. Unfortunately I don't know yet what to charge you, Ms. Garcia. I didn't get a report from Mr. Ruis."

"He called me. I don't have a written report either. That's perfectly okay."

"I don't understand."

"You satisfied your contract, Mr. Duvall. Mr. Ruis fulfilled your contract. He did his job well. I don't have to like it. Perhaps you don't know my friend Mr. Newton was murdered."

"I'm truly sorry, Ms. Garcia. I know what it means to lose a friend. In fact I'm calling because I seem to have misplaced Mr. Ruis."

"Now, I don't understand," she said.

"Mr. Ruis has been missing for at least a month. So far no one I have talked to has any idea where he is. He didn't file a report. I know this is a terrible time, but I'd like to interview you. He should have made progress reports to keep you informed. Perhaps I can learn something useful from you. Could you do that?"

I wasn't surprised by her long silence. Perhaps I was asking for more than she could give.

"I'm sorry to ask at such a difficult time, "I said. "Perhaps I should give you time to think about this, and call on you later."

"No reason to be sorry," she said. "Why don't you visit me tomorrow morning? Could you get here by 10:00?"

"Thank you, Ms. Garcia. I appreciate your effort. Could you give me directions about how to find your home?"

I dutifully wrote down her instructions. This was unnecessary of course. I could find it in any case, but she'd be more comfortable if she invited me by telling me how to find her.

"Thank you," I said. "You've made that very clear."

"Until tomorrow then," she said.

This could be a difficult interview, but I needed what this woman could tell me. I didn't think she could tell me where Tuco was, but that wasn't my only mystery. I'd know a lot more about Tuco's state of mind if I knew why he hadn't put in a claim for his work.

Floyd came home with company, an attractive lady named Sara who announced she was cooking his dinner.

I was amused. Floyd is probably a better cook than she is, and she was going to find his kitchen a bit of a shock.

Floyd lives in a wheelchair. His legs were blown off by a chicom claymore while he was carrying a M-60 for the 1/9th Marines, the Walking Dead. One of his stumps is too short for him to easily adapt to artificial limbs. He's been wheelchair bound for years.

Sara was going to find all of Floyd's spices and ingredients in no particular order on his counter tops where he could reach them.

I begged to be excused from dinner, but Floyd wanted to know about my morning with the El Sobrante cops. I told him about Dornacker's promise of efficient, equal service.

Floyd smiled. "I thought so. He really doesn't like you."

"Have a nice evening, Ms. Sara. I'm eating out," I said.

I headed for the bar at Chevy's near Hilltop Mall to give Floyd his evening with Sara. Maybe he was the better cook, but she didn't have to know that, and I had a hankering for the salt on the rim of a Margarita glass.

CHAPTER 8

I ate breakfast with Floyd and left with more than enough time to to reach Ms. Garcia's home in Petaluma. I drove to Vallejo and took Highway 37 west. There's always pretty substantial commute traffic on 37, but that thinned out when I turned north on the Lakeville Highway toward Petaluma.

I was in Petaluma too early so I stopped at a Starbucks and indulged myself with a latte' before I worked my way down the printout from Google Maps to Ms. Garcia's house just to the south of the downtown district.

The Garcia house was a small Victorian complete with gingerbread and a full surround porch. There was no separate garage, but a driveway ran from the street to a big carriage door on the north side of the house. Apparently this made a garage under porch. I would have bumped my head under that porch, but apparently it worked out for the current occupant, the driveway had tire tracks leading through the door.

There were few concessions to modernity besides the driveway. There was a stone wall around the property. A taller wrought iron fence ran against the inside of the wall with a gate opening to a walk to the porch and an automated sliding gate for the driveway. A new redwood ramp rose to the level of the porch from the sidewalk, and I could see another beyond the carriage door apparently leading to the back entrance.

I parked near the sidewalk gate. There was a small speaker cemented into the stone pillar to the right of the gate with a button. I pushed the button and heard a buzz.

I waited for some time, but the house was fairly large. Somewhere there was another speaker and another button. The resident could easily be some distance away.

Finally the box squawked. "Yes?"

"George Duvall, Ms. Garcia."

She buzzed me in.

The sidewalk to the porch was lined with young rose bushes, surely none of them more than a year or two old, but several now budding and soon to bloom.

I chose the steps instead of the ramp. The front door opened as I approached. I found I was looking down into brown eyes.

She was a striking woman; wings of dark hair framed a strong face, a Latina lady in her late 30's or early 40's, coffee and cream skin, a square jaw, full mouth, and a prominent but narrow nose. In my childhood I might have thought her an Indian princess. She nodded to me briefly, perhaps a remnant of a childhood curtsy, and shook my hand, smiling warmly.

"Mr. Duvall, I'm Teri Garcia. Please come in."

"Thank you."

Her brightly colored skirt, empty of legs, swung gracefully from the seat of her wheelchair as she turned left through the door to my right. A hundred years ago the room might have been a formal parlor. Now it was still arranged for guests, but hardly so formal.

"Have a seat. How else can I make you comfortable? Would you like some tea? Coffee? Perhaps a glass of water?"

She was courteous perhaps to a fault. "Water would be lovely," I said. "Thank you for seeing me."

"Not at all."

She turned away again, and wheeled down the central hallway behind the front door, presumably to the kitchen.

I thanked her silently for giving me a moment to steady my own composure. I deal fairly well with men who have been maimed. I've known a few. Women are more difficult, more disturbing than they should be. Maybe I'm a typical man of a certain age. I know I am not responsible, but my heart cries.

"Here we are, Mr. Duvall."

I seated myself in a cozy though erect wingback chair. She had brought a tray with a pitcher of iced water and a pair of glasses. She spread three coasters on the table between us, poured water over ice for the glass on my side, poured full her glass and placed the pitcher between, convenient to us both.

She smiled pleasantly. "How shall we begin?"

I decided this was not the time to act like a cop.

"Let me start by telling you again how sorry I am that you've lost your friend," I said.

She nodded. "Thank you. I knew I might lose him. I knew he was a damaged man, perhaps beyond repair, but that doesn't seem to make any difference. I shall miss him."

She looked down, I thought, to her missing legs.

"Much of life is managing loss. I've managed more than most. That which does not kill us makes us stronger. How can I help you today?"

"As I told you last night my friend, Tuco, has disappeared. The last job he did for me was to go looking for your friend. That can't be a coincidence."

"Certainly not," she said.

"Last night you said your friend Keith was murdered. If you don't mind would you tell me how you learned and when that happened?"

"Your friend Tuco told me. He came here to the house, maybe three weeks ago. He knew I would be concerned, he said. He thought it was important to learn the news from a friend rather than read about in it in some newspaper or see it on the news. He said he wanted to apologize. He considered it a personal failure."

Maybe Tuco was in a worse fix than I had thought. The cops had pulled the body out of the water only last Friday, but Tuco already knew or at least guessed that Newton was dead.

"Why a personal failure?" I asked.

"Well I think you already must know, that he found Keith and apparently got him out of a very tight spot. He just couldn't manage to keep him alive afterward."

"Actually," I told her. "I don't know a thing. I didn't know he found Mr. Newton. I didn't know any of the circumstances. I only learned the day before yesterday that Mr. Newton was dead. Tuco's supposed to file a report on his cases, but he hasn't given me one for you. I was hoping he gave you a copy. We try to provide that to every client."

She bit her lower lip. "Not exactly," she said.

"I don't understand."

"Well I thought you knew."

"What?

"I'm not exactly a client."

"I think I have a signed contract designating specific terms and conditions."

"Yes you do. I signed it. Tuco said it was what you wanted to let him walk around asking questions as your investigator."

"I don't understand."

"You were helping him set it up, he said. You told him it had to look as if there was a real client and a case."

"You were the client."

"Not really. If anybody was the client it was Tuco. Keith Newton was an old friend. Tuco knew him long before I did."

"He told me that. He said he had talked Newton out of suicide once."

"That's what he told me too."

"But you didn't hire him?"

"No. I helped him fake it because he said that's what you wanted him to do."

I was scratching my head now. Whatever I expected when I left the house, it wasn't this. Tuco, my so-called best friend, had conned me and conned this woman too. He had wanted to use my license as a cover for an investigation of his own.

When I thought about what he said to me, he'd almost told me the truth. "Lifetime favor," he said. Well why not? All he had to do was ask. Why the elaborate con?

"Maybe we could start at the other end," I said. "Keith Newton was a friend of yours."

"Yes. More or less. Originally he was my client."

Much of what she said next merely a fleshed out the details I already knew. Ms. Garcia was credentialed as a Marriage and Family Counselor, now in private practice here in her home. She had interned at a drug treatment facility where she had treated Keith Newton. Providing some pro bono care to needy veterans, she also volunteered at Foxhole where Newton had previously been both a client and an employee.

"Keith proposed to me once," she said.

"Did you think about it?"

"Briefly. Of course it would have been completely unethical. It's perfectly natural for a client to become attached to a therapist. We're taught to guard against that. I liked Keith quite a lot, but his proposal was just a way of expressing his neediness.

"There was a hole inside him that I was never going to fill, and I never did learn what could fill it. I just taught him that cocaine couldn't fill him either. He seemed to be an empty person, never quite finding meaning in life."

"But you cared about him?"

"He was somebody lost who was falling down."

"And Tuco, apparently cared about him too." I said.

"Your friend knew him long before I did."

"I didn't know Newton at all." I said. "Is there anything you can tell me about their friendship?"

She had met Tuco quite recently. When rumor came back to Foxhole that Newton disappeared again Foxhole staff called for a meeting of Newton's friends, Tuco among them. They were all concerned because of Newton's history with suicide. I could probably find out about that at Foxhole, she said.

At the Foxhole meeting they brainstormed how to track Newton down.

Once before Newton announced to friends he was going on a "Grand Farewell Tour". Then Tuco talked him out of suicide. He might again be visiting friends to say goodbye.

"Only he won't visit me," Tuco had said, "because he knows I'll hold him responsible."

Garcia asked Tuco how he did that. She still remembered quite vividly what Tuco said because she was impressed by it.

"This was his exact answer. He said (quote) I told him he'd be an inconsiderate asshole if he left behind a bloody mess for his friends. (Unquote.)"

"Yup," I said. "That's my kind and gentle friend, and I'll bet it really worked because Newton was a vet. I'll bet he saw some of those messes and had to clean them up."

"Very likely." Garcia said. "I've worked with a few combat vets. I'm good at it. I'm a veteran too. I lost my legs during Desert Storm."

"Welcome to the brotherhood of the blood," I said. "I served with Tuco in Vietnam. Tuco's got a lot of veteran friends," I said. "Looks as if he took some pretty big risks for Newton. Got any idea what made Newton special to him?"

"Only a glimpse," she said. "He said he was in a very tough spot a long time ago. He was a small time drug dealer and a much bigger and nastier guy wanted to take him out. He was getting counseling at Foxhole. Keith was in the group and taught him something special, Tuco said. Sometimes the only way out is through."

"As it happens," I said. "I know something about that. I know how it turned out. But let's get back to the present.

"Newton was missing and Tuco went looking for him apparently working a list of his friends."

"Yes, the gang at Foxhole made the list for him. Tuco called each of them up and if Keith had been there, he would get on his bike and go interview the guy."

"He finally called me from Stockton. Keith knew Tuco was looking for him and left a note for Tuco with a friend."

"Did Tuco read it to you?" I asked.

"Yes he did, but I don't remember it precisely. It was just a suggestion that they meet at the coffee shop in a marina on the Delta. I don't remember which one.

"The next day Tuco called about three o'clock in the afternoon to let me know he was in position. Keith called me about four, using Tuco's cell phone. He asked me to tell everybody he had a new job and he was fine."

"What was the point of that," I asked. "Now Tuco knew he wasn't going to kill himself."

She took a long drink from her water glass.

"That's a better question than you know," she said. "I don't have all the answers. At the time I thought we were still going through the rituals of your contract. He photographed Keith. He emailed me the picture. Keith phoned and we talked. Contract done.

"I thought that was an end to it, but actually things got worse. I'm not really clear about how. Apparently Keith's new boss was a very dangerous man and Tuco thought he had to pry Keith loose. I don't really have details. Some of the folks at Foxhole might.

"I saw Keith about four weeks ago down at Foxhole. Everything seemed fine. Then Tuco came and told me he was dead."

She'd talked freely, but seemed suddenly to stop.

I had a question in my head, but I couldn't bring myself to inflict it on her.

"I know how Keith died," I said. "I don't know why."

"Neither do I," she said firmly.

I tried to think of other questions I might ask, but nothing came to me. I drank more water. She had given me a possible lead. I would visit Foxhole and learn what I could.

I asked if she could let me have a photo of Keith Newton. What I got was a picture taken at a party. The picture was centered on Newton though there were many people around, most with a drink in hand. Newton had no drink. His hands were clasped loosely before him, all of his attention on the face of the woman whose back was to the camera. He was grinning, head tilted slightly, and one eyebrow was arched dramatically as if in doubt. He had a wonderful grin, devilish, a prankster full of fun, but with some furtive cruelty in it.

I thanked Ms. Garcia for her time, told her I might call on her again and I assured her that there would never be a bill.

I don't care how Tuco spends his own time. If there were no reports the only evidence there had ever been a case was my scattered file, half at home and half in storage.

CHAPTER 9

When I got back to Floyd's place Tuesday about noon, I spent some time on the telephone. I got lucky when I called Foxhole. They were in mourning and eager to talk about Keith Newton.

I spoke with the director, Gary Workman, who, I was surprised to learn, thought of Tuco as one of the shelter's better friends. He was quite concerned when I told him that Tuco might be in some kind of trouble.

"He never forgot his time here. He was grateful for our help, and gave back to us often and in creative ways. I made up the list of Keith's friends for Tuco. In these circumstances I'm sure that none of them would mind hearing from you. Give me your email address and I'll send it to you."

"I'd also like to meet with you directly," I said. "Perhaps I could address several of you at once? Is there a weekly staff meeting?"

"Certainly. We have a staff meeting on Fridays at 10:30. I'll put you first on the agenda.

"Friday at 10:30. You're still in that storefront on San Pablo?"

"Same old shop," he said. "We're in the book."

"I'll see you then."

Within minutes I had Gary's list. There were only a couple of guys in Stockton.   One of them might know the Marina where Tuco and Newton met. Since Newton died out there, it would be another step closer to the truth.

Early in the afternoon Floyd came back to the cottage to cadge a beer, and we traded the stories of our day so far.

He stared at the picture of Newton for a long time.

"A sad man," he said.

"You see that in the picture?"

"Maybe not the picture. Maybe it don't mean anything, but I think I've met him."

"Might help if you remembered where," I said.

"I'll think about it," Floyd said.

"I'd appreciate it," I said. "I've got group at four, but you can stay here and drink as much of the Poleeko Gold as you like."

Group always starts the same. Al leads the prayer. We say Amen and then one at a time we check in. Most guys start saying they're doing fine, but pretty quick you find out if they're not. Most talk about what they said before, and if there's a real blowup you hear about it right off the bat.

Al said, "So tell us what happened this week, George."

By now I had a lot practice summing up Tuco's disappearance. It was easy. Since these guys were veterans I told them the word was on the street to look for Cav guys from a Recon platoon.

"I had to come today," I said. "I hoped he'd show up."

The group had a lot to add, talking all at once, some speeches stepping on the others.

"Lots of Cav guys on the streets," said a guy that had served in the 5/7th.

"Not so many Recon, though," said the retired CSM who served with the 9th.

"And few here, the East Bay, Alameda or Contra Costa County," Tom said.

"We never, ever get away," said a personnel exec from HP.

"Nor do you really want to," Al said.

"Once you think you put the Nam behind you, it rears up and bites you in the ass," said a guy from black ops with MACSOG.

"We're just God's new chosen people."

"Born to suffer."

"Our lot in life."

"Bullshit. We're still here."

"None of you have yet met that bullet with your name on it."

"Duvall and I talked," Al said. "Things came up. I thought I should ask here. You all can see how close Duvall and Tuco are. Anyone else like that? Anyone else still tight with some guy he went through the Nam with?"

"Me. Michael's in Michigan. Every year at Tet, I call him up and we talk about nothing much. I just want to know he's there. We celebrate being alive."

"I ain't seen none of those bastards since."

"A guy in my Company had some old orders and looked us all up on the Internet. There's a reunion every year, usually close to the Division reunion. I hadn't laughed or cried so much in years."

"But I don't hear anybody close like Tuco and Duvall, almost living together like being married or something."

"Hell, I don't tell the real stuff to my wife. It's not like being married."

"Tom, you're awful quiet," Al said. "Something on your mind?"

Tom leaned forward rubbing his hands as if to wash them without soap or water.

"My first trip to the wall. My young friend Malikah graduated from Fisk. I'd been to her commencement. General Powell spoke. Malikah's mother had business in Washington, and I had an agency meeting. We met at the Memorial."

Tom folded his hands leaned back and looked up at the ceiling through moist eyes..

"I'd seen the traveling wall, but it's not the same. I think it's about the way the stone rises from the ground, biggest damn tombstone ever, made for all the men we'll never meet again."

Cheeks wet, Tom smiled.

"Malikah and I thought I was doing pretty well. I was cool. I was keeping it together. The guardians at the wall are all old grunts like us, each in some uniform of his choice, some outward sign, jungle fatigues on one, a boony hat on another, several with a Division Patch, each declaring in his own way that he'd made the long damned trip with us.

"Midway down at the belly of the wall, a grizzled grunt grabbed a young girl leaning over the wall, almost dangling too far down from the top.

"'Don't', he said; 'You'll fall.'"

"Next to me a short guy said.'I was just trying to get a rubbing of my brother's name.'

"Well I'm a tall guy. Six foot three inches last time I looked. I could fix the problem. Piece of cake."

Tom smiled broadly, somehow amused at his own naiveté.

"Is that the name? I asked the short guy, pointing with my finger where the girl had reached. He nodded yes.

"They hand out paper for rubbings with large leaded pencils for the families at the wall. I took his, paper in my left, pencil in right, and reached up with both hands to the name of one I never knew."

Briefly, Tom bowed his head forward now as if in prayer, and then he straightened, spoke again looking each of us in the eye.

"Stretching to the top of my reach, I felt my hands pressing against the wall, its size and weight, suddenly crushing and enormous. One more time for just one more task, I was reaching out, giving support, and comfort to a long dead brother.

"I may have cried for an hour. Malikah took care of me.

"Death binds us," Tom said after some silence.

Al turned to me. "Death binds you and Tuco too. I need know nothing more, but maybe you do."

"I don't think so, Al. I know what I know. It don't mean nothing."

CHAPTER 10

I got back to Floyd's place late. The van wasn't parked outside when I arrived. Floyd was still enjoying his social life. I decided to wait for him at least a little while.

I shut the garage door from the outside and grabbed a lawn chair on Floyd's porch.

Two doors down to the right, a guy was washing his car in the fading light. I could see Floyd's neighbor across the way through open curtains where he sat watching television with his wife. Down the street four or five guys were working on the engine of some muscle car. In this neighborhood that counts as a quiet night.

After half an hour I called Floyd on his cell.

"It's George," I said. "Are you getting home soon?"

"In about five minutes," Floyd said.

"Thanks. I'd like my pistol from your gun safe. I want to clean it and check it out."

"You leave it dirty?"

"No of course not. You just can't check too often or too well."

"Relax Duvall. Go back to your place and pour us a couple of cold ones. I like that Poleeko Gold stuff you picked up. I'll bring your gun around back."

I couldn't figure why I was feeling jumpy. I got up and strolled out front to the sidewalk looking left and right. Nothing new and nothing had changed. I let myself in the side gate and took the narrow path between the garage and the fence back to my studio cottage.

After a while Floyd rolled into the cottage in his chair with my pistol case on his lap. He took a long pull from the glass of Poleeko Gold I poured for him and held the cold condensate against the sweat shining on the dark skin of his forehead. "Lovely," he said.

It was still a little warm, but I closed the door. While Floyd watched I clamped my desk lamp to the dining table. I centered the lamp's arm over the table at the height of my head, bathing the table in white, bright light. I covered the table with newspaper, stripped the gun, laid out the parts. I began to use solvent, rags, and gun oil, under the bright lamp to clean, examine, and lubricate each moving part.

"Lighten up, Duvall," Floyd said. "Enjoy some beer."

"There's pleasure in this too," I said. Still I wiped my hands and poured another glass.

"Lovely indeed."

"No sense getting worked up; there's no bogey man here," Floyd said.

"No bogey man yet!" I said. I resumed my work with the glass at hand.

He chuckled. "Don't you worry, boy. You're in my house. I'm going to take care of you."

"Maybe I should move out."

"You nervous? Are you hyped up? You haven't woken me rudely in the night the way you did your wife."

"But maybe somebody would."

"Maybe, maybe not. Don't get me wrong. Clean up that gun and go to the range. Make sure you still know what you're doing. There's nothing wrong with that. Be ready. Just remember you always are. Keep your head screwed on right. Be watchful, but be relaxed. Stay cool and be ready."

I'd begun to reassemble the gun when the door of the cottage cracked, bowed, and broke open. I hurried. My nickname's Blondie, but I'm not as fast as the guy in the movie.

A big ugly man followed the broken door into the room. How was he ugly? Let me count the ways. One thing was the.357 Magnum in his right hand.

My gun was still in pieces in my hands.

"Well, well, well!" he snickered. "It's the nigger loving cop and his gimp nigger friend. Family time at gimp nigger's house."

Floyd put down his beer.

The thug leered, stuck out his tongue, and waved it at us. He was at least two inches taller than I am. He looked to outweigh me by at least a hundred pounds. His head was shaved and shaped like a bowl turned upside down. There was a small swastika about half an inch wide tattooed by amateurs at the crown of his right cheekbone just below his eye.

We were in for an ugly time.

"I've got the gun, but nobody's asked me what I fucking want," he said. "You," he pointed at me with a nod of his head. "Get behind your friend and grab onto the back of his chair."

I moved and grabbed.

Now the bullet from that heavy gun could easily pass through both Floyd and me.

"Don't bother looking at the telephone. I've cut the line. Where is Tuco Ruis?"

"We don't know." I said.

"Well that's too bad, honey. I can't just take your word for it."

"I'll start here because it will feel so good." He shifted the gun to his left hand, but the muzzle never wavered. He reached out with his right hand, slapped Floyd hard enough to turn his head, and bloodied Floyd's nose with a backhand fist.

"Maybe we'll have some more fun, honey, when I've finished with your friend." He lifted his eyes from Floyd's face to mine. "Turn around," he said, and when I hesitated in sing song said, "I've still got the gu-un!"

Turning was one of the hardest things I've ever done. I was abandoning Floyd, but there was nothing I could do. I felt more vulnerable too. I couldn't see the bastard. I couldn't see what was coming.

I heard two more vicious blows. "That's just to keep you warm, honey. Stay right there. I'll be back and we'll have some fun. I ain't had me a gimp nigger in years."

I saw him next out the corner of my right eye. He was circling about five feet away. He was thinking, staying so far away that I couldn't make a play for the gun, but acting casual about it. The muzzle of the weapon had dropped, but was still in easy position to shoot either of us or both. I was astonished when he lay the pistol down on the kitchen counter next to the sink.

"I don't think I need this, honey," he said and began to punch.

I have good reactions for a man my age. I ducked some blows. I slid inside of others. He was still too big. I slipped inside a roundhouse right, his forearm still stunned me. My reactions were fast, but his were faster. I'm becoming an old man. I couldn't take this for long. Maybe the best way out was to let myself lose more quickly.

He got a good blow to my gut, I groaned and drew that round house right again. I helped. I turned with the punch and fell, sprawling out to his left, no longer behind Floyd, but beside him.

Ugly was smart enough to pick up the gun. "Tuco Ruis?"

It seemed quite pointless to answer him.

He kicked me in the solar plexus. I rolled away moaning, struggling for breath, and grateful he'd missed my ribs.

He followed me with another kick to my back as I rolled away. "Tuco Ruis?

The gunshot was deafening in the small apartment, but the shrill shriek that followed continued long after the shot died away.

"Lookee, lookee," Floyd said, spitting away the blood from his nose as it spilled over his mouth and chin. "The gimp nigger's got a gun."

I knew of course; his H&K 9 is always there, hidden under the remains of his right thigh in his wheel chair.

The shrieking continued. The big man collapsed on his left side, grabbing at what was left of his knee, though incredibly still waving around that damned cannon.

Another gunshot and more screaming.

"Asshole! You got no knees left, and I've got several more rounds. You keep waving that thing around and I'm going to be more justifiably in fear of my life."

I staggered to my feet, stomped on asshole's gun hand, and kicked away the cannon.

"Floyd, call the cops on your cell," I croaked. "He's probably busted mine."

Turns out I was wrong. My cell phone still worked.

El Cerrito P.D. was quick and for the most part good. Asshole had an ambulance, handcuffs, and a uniformed escort within minutes. Floyd packed his nose with gauze and made us both ice packs.

Only one of the cops was a jerk.

"Why did you shoot him twice," the cop asked Floyd.

"Because he still had his gun and he was threatening my friend."

"Yes, he was," I said.

"Where was your gun hidden, sir?"

"I told you. Under my thigh in my wheelchair."

"Do you always carry?"

"In my own house."

"And why did you have it there tonight."

"Because there are racist assholes. One got quite nasty before you got here."

"In your own house?"

"Sometimes. Tonight, for instance. I've got no way of knowing where they're going to be."

"Do you always carry your gun there out of the house?"

"Why, officer don't you know that's illegal. A misdemeanor, I believe."

"I know."

"So why do you ask?"

"I want you to confess your crime."

"Thank you very much," Floyd said. "Perhaps I'm not fully aware of the risks. Maybe you'd better arrest me next time."

They glared at each other.

They took Floyd's H&K, for ballistics they said. Since my Kimber was not yet assembled they left it with me. I had a word with the chief investigating officer before he took off.

"Do you know who I am?"

"Sure, Chief Duvall. I've been working here down the road from you for about fifteen years."

"I think of your boss as my friend. Would you tell him I'll be asking questions about your results? He can decide what he's willing to tell me."

"No problem. But I'm surprised you want to ask. You and I both know in advance because we know his brand of skinhead and its turf covers both of our towns. At a guess this was an initiation. If he got answers he got to be a soldier. If he got cooked he clearly wasn't a fit member of the Aryan race."

"Thanks Detective."

"Not a problem. In fact my pleasure. I'll fill the Chief in on details, and like you said..."

"Thanks again."

A reporter for the West Contra Times showed up. I told him I was confident in the El Cerrito P.D. and I was sure their investigation was ongoing. He left me and headed for the house, probably to see what he could get out of Floyd.

I told the crime scene guys they could have most of the room. They supervised me as I packed a few things and headed out the door.

I stopped for a moment in Floyd's house. The reporter had left. Floyd had cleaned up pretty good. His nose had stopped bleeding. His left eye was a little swollen and would probably blacken some more, but he was in very good spirits.

He offered me a high five, which from Floyd came in about the height of my shoulder. "We still got it."

"Any place, any time, Floyd. You yell, and I'll come running."

"We make a good team Duvall. There was no way I could get around in time for a shot if you hadn't moved him."

"Sorry about your gun."

"That's okay." He reached under his thigh and brought out another H&K 9. "Backup," he said.

"He needed shooting Floyd.

"There's a nice hotel near the Hilltop Mall with a security patrol. I'll spend the night there and maybe come back when they release the scene. Thanks again."

"No problem."

At the hotel I poured myself bruises and all into their sauna and afterward their whirlpool.

Sitting on the bed, I called Lily before I turned in. It was late at night, but better she should hear it from me than on the news.

"Hello."

"Hi sugar lumps. I'm calling to make a report."

"Can't it wait 'til morning?"

"I don't think so. I don't want you to read about this first in the newspaper."

"What happened?"

"A skinhead with a gun barged in on Floyd and me tonight."

"You guys okay?"

"Fine. Lumps, bruises, and maybe swollen pride."

"That doesn't sound so bad."

"Not for us, but Floyd put a couple of holes in the skinhead. I think the papers may make it sound more exciting. A reporter talked to Floyd and I bet he'll be all over the decals on Floyd's chair."

Floyd's decorated his wheelchair with decals, the USMC emblem and the Vietnam Service Ribbon among them.

"Just so long as you're okay."

"I haven't told you everything yet, sweetie. There's something that probably won't make the paper."

"Okay. What?"

"The skinhead was there to ask me about Tuco." I paused and let her take that in.

"We were right. He is in trouble."

"Maybe we all are. Bob Schooner says the word on the street is to look out for 1st Cav guys from a Recon platoon."

"Oh." After a moment she chuckled. "I guess I'm going to be okay."

"Not if you live in my house. He was there to ask me."

"Well good. At least he knew you weren't at home."

"Maybe not good enough. Why don't you call Karen and ask her if you can sleep over for a few nights."

"Okay. I'll do that. First thing in the morning."

"Thank you, sweetheart. I'll sleep better. Good night."

I'd had more than enough for one day, but I wasn't quite ready for bed.

I looked through the call log on my cell phone, found the 414 number, selected it and pushed the green send button.

If it was late at night for me, it was later at night for him. To hell with it. His turn for disturbed sleep.

He answered grumpy," Yeah?"

"El Tee is that you?"

"Huh? Who the hell is this?"

"Blondie. It's me, Blondie. Remember what I called about the other day?"

"Yeah. I remember. I'm awake now."

"Things have gotten hairy. I was in a scuffle with a goon. He had a gun. He was looking for Tuco Ruis. There was some shooting. Did you find out anything?"

"About what?"

I couldn't get pissy about his memory. It was probably two or three in the morning wherever he was. "About Tuco's disappearance. Has he talked to anybody? Does anybody know anything?"

"No. Nothing. Not about that. Nobody's said anything about that. But there's something maybe you should know."

"Something?"

He yawned into the phone. "I gotta tell you. So far just a little more than rumor. I'll find out more. So far I've talked to guys who have talked to guys. The CID is definitely sniffing around, asking questions about January 1971. This isn't a rumor anymore."

Days ago I would have blown him off, but he had my full attention now.

"You know," he said, "the night of the pigs."

I took a pause and then asked. "What about it?"

For a long moment my only answer was silence. "Give me a fucking break, Blondie. I was there too."

An isolated platoon is far worse than a small town. How can you keep a secret? I had done my best. I still felt sure of 2nd squad's loyalty, but maybe they weren't the only ones to guess. The El Tee had been arranging his reunions. I thought of all those men as friends, but I wouldn't want to guess what they said.

"What do you think you know, Bookman?"

"I know that you and Tuco are the closest of friends."

There was no reason to share my personal recent doubts.

"I know that I told the two of you, that the old lady was your responsibility, and I know what I know I don't want to know."

I managed to speak in an even tone. "Enemy fire, sir."

He laughed. "Son, don't try to tell the liar that he's told the truth. I was there, remember? Who did you think made that up?

"Listen, Duvall. If Tuco's really missing, you've got to find him. If there's really somebody out to get you, maybe the only chance you've got is to back each other up. I'm sure you're tough enough to fend off questions. At least you used to be; you were the strength for both of you."

Maybe I still was. Without me, Tuco might be dead. Ghost would have crushed him twenty years before.

"Don't sweat this," the El Tee said. "You didn't hear any of this from me, and that's certainly not what I'm going to say to anybody official. We've all been through much tighter scrapes. Find our friend. I'll help in any way I can."

"Thanks, El Tee."

"No sweat, Blondie. I'll let you know if I find anything out. Now let me go back to sleep."

He might have slept soundly. I know I did not.

CHAPTER 11

I slept in Thursday morning, waking around 8:30, stiff and bruised.   The only unbruised parts of me were ribs that hadn't been kicked. My cell phone was ringing.

"George Duvall," I answered.

"This is Schooner," he said. "Just read the morning reports, I see you've met my apprentice gang banger."

"The guy Floyd shot last night?"

"Yeah."

"When you spoke of him the other day he didn't seem quite so...motivated?"

Schooner laughed. "He knows me. I guess he didn't know you, and for sure he didn't know Floyd!"

"Thanks for calling, Bob."

"No problem. I knew you'd want to know. How's it going so far?"

I told him I had filed the missing persons report, and I briefed him on Garcia's story and the mysterious origins of the Newton case.

"What's your next step?"

"I've got a date to interview the staff at Foxhole."

"Well keep me in the loop," Schooner said.

"What about Glowery? Is he on to me yet?"

"He knows you're Tuco's friend and might know where he is. He probably has watched you a bit and knows you're looking. I don't think he knows you're looking for me. He probably thinks you're on your own."

"Maybe in this case a distinction without a difference," I said.

"You can watch your own back, Duvall. I'm looking the other way and whistling a happy tune."

I hung up the phone rather than cuss him out.

I shaved and took a quick shower. I got a robe on and went looking for the ice machine. I probably spent half an hour in bed and icing my bruised arms.

By now it was approaching 11:00 o'clock. I had to hustle a little to get myself together and out of the room.

I drove back to El Sobrante and had breakfast at El Soleil. That late in the morning there were few booths. I ate at the counter, and read the papers, West Contra Costa Times and the San Francisco Chronicle.

The Chronicle mentioned nothing about our little incident of the night before.

The Times story was several paragraphs. The skinhead a.k.a. Mattias Brownstein had been taken to Brookside emergency under guard. The assault was described as a home invasion. The El Cerrito P.D. investigation was ongoing. I was named as the former Chief in El Sobrante; Floyd was mentioned and the decals on his wheelchair were described.

The reporter in his final paragraphs had some fun. He suggested our assailant was foolish to go up against two combat veterans, had he but known. There was more ink about Floyd's decorated combat service and his unflinching pride.

I noticed off hand that a couple of guys slid into the seats on either side of me, but I paid no special attention until one of them spoke to me.

"Lucky, Chief Duvall."

I looked up from my paper to my left. Nowadays he dressed in suits and had shaved away not only his beard and mustache but also sideburns. He'd slimmed down a lot too. I was probably one of few men in the room who knew there was likely a forest of biker tattoos under Claude Hodiak's Italian silk.

He wasn't a guy I wanted to see.

"Thank you, Mr. Hodiak. I'm happy to win on luck. I'm not young anymore. I'm no longer sure of skill."

Hodiak surprised me with a generous smile. "I share your pain."

Behind me now to the right another voice said, "It probably helped that the guy was pretty stupid."

I turned back to identify the new voice. I didn't know him. His suit fit pretty well, but I'd bet he hadn't been shaving as long as Claude. "How's that," I said.

"If they really wanted the two of you, why send one guy?"

"I don't think you have the picture quite right sir. I don't think 'they" cared one way or the other. Brownstein probably wasn't yet in with the wolf pack. If he got something from me, swell. If he didn't and does his time, it costs them nothing, and now maybe I'm running scared."

"Just like the old days," Hodiak said. "This ain't a social call. Mr. Glowery would like to see you."

Of course it'd be Ghost; Hodiak was his right hand man.

"Would I like to see him? This may surprise you, but it's been years."

"Why not? If he wanted to hurt you, would he send me?"

No he wouldn't. Hodiak was Glowery's chief executive; like his boss he was now kept well away from the rough stuff.

"Okay," I said. "Can this be now or do I need to make an appointment."

"He's expecting you."

"Fine, but I'll drive my own car."

"That's acceptable," Hodiak said. "I'll escort you in mine."

I felt pretty safe since he was letting me drive unaccompanied. I've got a Blue-tooth headset. Once I was behind the wheel, I talked to my cell phone and called Mark Vinson. I got his voice-mail.

"Vinnie this is Duvall. It's about eleven o'clock Thursday morning. I've been invited out to Glowery's house. Probably no big deal. So far as we know, he's never done anything on our turf. Still if I haven't called you back by one o'clock, send the cavalry."

With the picture of Newton's mangled body in my head, I didn't think this was an idle precaution.

Glowery's place is back in the hills on the north side of the Dam Road canyon. I'd never want to live there. There's a thick wood of scrub oak that will catch fire one day, and burn very hot. Like any good trap, it's also well defended. There's only one street in, also of course the only street out.

Maybe Glowery thought that was good, until Tuco showed him one could come in the back door.

One night long ago when I was the brand new Chief of Police in El Sobrante, Tuco asked for my help. He told me he needed to confront Glowery, but he wouldn't tell me why. He asked me to drive a city cruiser and wait for him in front of Glowery's cul-de-sac.

At the time I hadn't seen Tuco for ten years. After he got out of the hospital, he had jumped on his Harley and drove off to find America. I hadn't heard a word from him until he asked me to wait in front of Glowery's house. I was sure this wasn't a good thing, but I didn't know how it was a bad thing and I was careful not to ask.

I sat there watching for Tuco in my rear view mirror, when he suddenly appeared from the front in clothing and a camo painted face. He had sneaked into Glowery's house from the back side, entered from a crawl space in a closet, head whacked Glowery's body guards and confronted their boss.

He gave Glowery the names and addresses of his first level weed pushers. "If they're still there," Tuco told him. Glowery could have them and his whole dope business – if any of the pushers were dumb enough to still be doing it. Glowery was welcome if he could find anything left.

Meanwhile the local Chief of Police, me, George Duvall, was waiting outside to pick him up, and what exactly did Glowery intend to do about it?

Glowery's security had improved since Tuco's night visit. He walled the place, at least in front. To get to the front door you pass a guard in a shack. I could only assume he had improved the back. An assault up the hill where Tuco sneaked into the house would be difficult and therefore unlikely from the hoods most likely to give Glowery trouble. For those he need only watch the road where his guard was posted.

Now the guards are professionals, uniformed guys with billed caps and holstered side arms, a name brand security company. Ghost owns a piece of it, and controls it through a shell corporation. Mostly the security company guards him or his companies, so much so the FBI suggested companies were controlled by Glowery if they used his guards.

I parked the Z3 on the street, just as Hodiak knew I would. With my car on the street I preserved an illusion that I was free to go.

"Thank you, Chief" Hodiak said. "Mr. Glowery is waiting to receive us."

"Us?"

"Donald and I will accompany you."

"This is Chief Duvall," he told the guard at the front gate.

"Lean against the wall," the guard said. "I need to pat you down."

"No need," I said, opening my jacket, "Here's my gun."

He reached for it and I slapped his wrist.

"I'm invited. I keep the gun. Call inside and see if he wants me in there or not."

"Never mind," said Hodiak.

Stepping back into his booth, the guard buzzed us through

Barefoot dressed in a dark blue silk robe, Glowery met me on the flagstone walkway, offering an open hand. I knew he was a couple of years younger than me, but he didn't look a day over day over 49.

"There you are, Blondie. How's it hanging? I can barely remember the last time we spoke."

"I remember clearly," I said. "It was my special day, my last in the bush. I was saying goodbye to everyone in the platoon."

"Really that long ago?"

"Really. Oh I know you've been in town, but you've never dropped in and I never felt like it. Only my oldest friends call me Blondie anymore. You can call me Duvall."

"Come in; come in," he said.

Hodiak and Donald took up seats near the door. Glowery stepped behind a mini bar

"Might I offer coffee or tea? Hot or iced? It's too early I'm sure for me to offer you, a stalwart of the law, a drink. I'm having tea."

The room was a marvel I did not expect, a bright white carpet and Danish modern furniture but for the big leather recliner opposite an immense flat screen television hung on an arm from a wall.

"Maybe I'm not so stalwart as I used to be," I said. "Maybe I've always been less stalwart than you imagine. It seems to be much later in my morning than in yours. I'd be happy to have a beer."

He smiled as if at some secret pleasure, pulled a cold Poleeko Gold from the bar refrigerator and poured it into a chilled glass.

I accepted somewhat warily and took a sip. He was pouring my brand. I'd been watching him for many years; he'd been watching me too. Maybe the Ghost knew more about me than I knew about him, though what I knew or believed about him wasn't very nice.

Glowery made tea with the grace of Ghost's silent jungle moves. He put a container of tea leaves with great precision in alignment with the edge of the bar. He carefully opened the package, measured tea leaves into a small silver infuser, snapped the cover shut, and languidly stirred the infuser in a cup of hot steaming water.

"Have a seat," he said, waving me toward a couch. Donald and Hodiak remained standing behind me at the door. Ghost sat in the recliner but did not tilt back. There was an end table by the chair, but he chose to hold his saucer on his lap and sip tea now and then.

The couch seemed flimsy and narrow and thinly padded compared to Ghost's chair. He'd given himself a throne but only temporary seating for guests.

I sprawled back on the couch and propped my beer glass against my leg between sips.

"We've come a long way," he said.

"Long time ago," I said. "Lots of time to change or forget."

"I didn't forget," Ghost said. "I don't think I've changed all that much either."

Probably not. In Vietnam he was always cool and detached. I had admired that in those circumstances, but here it repelled me. He spoke the forms of courtesy, but with no feeling, not even the false feeling of the too practiced host. He'd offered me Poleeko Gold just to watch me squirm.

"I'll get right to the point," Ghost said. "I hear maybe you're looking for Tuco Ruis."

No point in denying it. I hadn't been trying to hide it. Ghost probably knew a twisted cop somewhere who had noticed my missing person's report.

"An old friend," I said.

"Who one night held a sawed off shotgun on me while you sat outside in darkness waiting in a car."

"I heard about that after the fact," I said. "He'd told me to wait. I didn't know what he planned. I'd have had to stop it if he'd told me. Legally that was assault, though you filed no complaint."

"Would it have mattered if I had? I doubt it. You'd have backed him. You always did. In the Nam I never saw one of you without the other. Tuco Ruis is the only man who ever stood up against me. Successfully that is.

"I want to hire you. I want you to find Tuco Ruis."

"Never mind. I'll find him," I said, "but I won't sell him to you. Was it something he said? Why do you want him?"

"For many years I never thought of Tuco but with that shotgun. I kept it as a souvenir. Have a look."

He pulled a sawed off pump from under the bar and put it down on top.

"I never thought I'd see him again," he said.

"Long time ago," I said. "We were young then. If you haven't messed with him since, why do you want him now?"

Glowery put his cup and saucer on the end table and sat back in his chair.

"I've wondered about you," he said, ignoring my question. "That night Tuco and me made a kind of bargain. I had his operation, what was left of it. I wouldn't kill him because you'd come after me. He said you were loyal to each other in a way I could understand. I knew you as partners in war. He'd guarantee to stay out of my business and he'd guarantee that you would too. If I didn't make messes in your town, you'd leave me alone."

"Now was that your bargain or just his?"

"I try to make bargains with no one but myself," I said. "I find that I am the only one who knows when my word is good. On the other hand, Tuco knows me well. He knows I won't borrow trouble and he could safely promise I wouldn't."

"That's the two of you," Glowery said. "Each of you looking out for the other all the time. Startling, really. You're such different people. I almost envy you. You're disciplined, loyal, and steadfast. The kind of guys you ought to be able to trust."

"I used to think so," I said.

"I used to think so too, but he didn't stay out of my business."

"Maybe you didn't stay out of his. Maybe you could tell me about it."

"That's a little tricky," Glowery said. "You still carry a badge."

"It says 'Retired' on it."

"If I was to confess to a crime you might feel the need

to try to arrest me."

"Foolish in the current circumstances."

"Perhaps even deadly."

"Perhaps to more than one of us."

"Perhaps."

He was still just a thug. Glowery's threats were quite real; his elegance and delicacy took nothing away from that. I knew the legend from the intelligence file. He began his criminal career, as a hanger on of a small biker gang, but Glowery was always willing to do what seemed unlikely, in this case something so disgusting that even his fellow gang bangers wouldn't – rob old Chinese graves out in the Delta to recover antique opium buried with the dead.

"Tuco swore he'd stay out of my business," Glowery said.

"There was always a condition," I said. "Whether he said so or not, that you'd stay out of his."

"I didn't touch him. I wouldn't. I knew about the two of you."

"What did you know?"

"With you it was always all for one and one for all."

"We didn't wear any fancy plumed hats."

Glowery laughed. "That'd be one way to get shot at for sure. It was never that way for me. It was just a big kick. I learned a lot though. I run a shop far more military than you might expect. I'm big on discipline. My guys do exactly what I tell 'em. Don't you boys?"

"Yes boss," Hodiak said. He nodded cautiously, and Donald nodded with him.

"I'm sure your discipline is very strict," I said.

"Count on it," said Glowery. "I'm as tough as they come."

"Okay."

"Does the name Keith Newton mean anything to you?" Glowery asked.

"It does now."

"It should. He was another damned grunt, a former

Marine. He worked for me. Worked out real good until your buddy, Tuco showed up. Newton calls me and tells me Tuco's a buddy of his, and from what he has heard, not too bad in a tough situation."

Glowery stood up, picked up his cup and saucer, walked behind the bar, and fiddled with the lid of an electric tea kettle, apparently checking how full it was. He pushed a button on the base to heat the water again.

I watched and waited.

"I listened to Newton's story very carefully." Glowery said. "He wasn't being a wise ass. He was way too trusting and sincere. My guess was Tuco never told him about busting into my place. Maybe he never told him anything about knowing me at all. I asked him straight up if Tuco knew he'd be working for me.

"Newton said Tuco knew and didn't care. Newton said he told Tuco the job was riding shotgun on stuff we were taking to Mexico. Newton said that was okay with Tuco, just so long as it was a load into Mexico and not from it."

"Tuco might say that," I said. "So you let our old war buddy in?"

"Welcomed him with open arms. Let bygones be bygones, I said. I knew I could use a man with his skills."

"Then it's old soldiers home week, beer, whiskey, and party time with a couple of broads. Newton and Tuco are all the time trying to top each other with fucking war stories. Almost made me puke."

Glowery got out his chair, walked back to the bar and made another cup of tea.

"You were in on the party?"

"It was my party. It's my island."

The Chinese graves where Glowery started were from a fishing village out in the San Joaquin Delta. After he started making real money, he bought an island out there. Folks outside of California don't know much about the Delta, but then most folks in California don't know much. It's wild country surrounded by cities yet remote and inaccessible. In the sixties it was rumored one farmer kept illegals as slaves on his island where they couldn't get off.

Much of the Sacramento valley was first a wetland drained for farmland or filled by the sediment during the California gold rush. The Delta is all that's left of that big wetland. After the transcontinental railroad was completed, many of the Chinese workers who built the railway turned their strong backs to building a system of levees to reclaim the rich land of the Delta. The waterway through the delta is a maze of sloughs and channels. Bridges and ferryboats link much of it, but there are still islands that can only be accessed by water or air. Glowery's was one of them.

"Well I hope you all had a very good time," I said.

"A swell time until morning."

"Hangover?"

"A major god damned headache that I've still got."

"Still."

"Newton and your asshole buddy were both gone. So was my load, several thousand pounds of it in a Ford Econoline Van."

"From the island?"

"No better place to hide it," Glowery said. "And no way to drive off. I own the only boat I know of that could carry it out, a ferry. I still don't know how they did it, but I want to. And I want my fucking van back too. I want my van; I want to collect my fucking money." He smacked the top of the bar with the flat of his hand.

"This didn't happen overnight," I said. "Newton's dead."

"I heard that," he said smiling.

"Tuco was at my place until Newton got killed."

"I knew that too."

"If I got the timing right, Newton wasn't killed for some time after he got clear of you."

"Correct but irrelevant. There's no way you can prove I had anything to do with his death."

"I can see you've been very patient."

"I've been patient too long."

I grinned but tried very hard not to laugh. "Let me guess," I said. "Newton and Tuco disappeared and you didn't know which of them had your stuff or where. You knew where Tuco was. My place. You'd prefer not to mess with us, so you went on a hunt for Newton. It's just my guess, but I think you found him. To rattle Tuco's cage you told him about it. Tuco wouldn't hang around my house and put my woman in danger so he finally left.

"If anybody knows where your stuff is, Tuco does, but he slid out too fast.

"You don't know what to do or where to look, and then you hear that I'm looking too. You could have just watched me like you watched everybody else, but you decided it'd be more fun to lean on me.

"You shoulda called a cop," I said. "Might be a felony rap if your stuff was worth enough."

"I called a goddamn cop," Glowery said. "You've still got a badge even if it says retired on it. Maybe you won't take my money, but you'll find him. If you find him, I find him; when I find him he's going to tell me where he put it."

"You might have to come through me first," I said.

"That won't be hard," Glowery said, "I could bury you now. I could still take you by myself, Blondie, but I don't have to; I've got competent backup."

"Claude," Glowery said, "give us the room. He won't give me any trouble."

Back at the bar he dropped his hand to the stock of the shotgun.

My mouth felt very dry.

"Not a good idea," I said. "I might not be the only one to get hurt. Hurt or dead, I'll do a poor job of finding Tuco."

Glowery nodded at his men, "Go."

They left.

"Just so you know I'm serious," he said.

"No doubt of it."

"There's another good reason not to kill you."

"Well sure," I said. "I'm guessing you wouldn't want to stain this nice carpet."

"If I killed you Tuco'd be after me. After the evening he spent here, I have to respect that."

I nodded. "There's a corollary you seem to have missed. What do you think will happen if you take out Tuco?"

"Oh you might try," Glowery said, "but I think your long service to the law would limit you."

"Good to see you're not just a simple hood."

"Certainly not; I'm a libertarian."

"Excuse me?"

"I'm a businessman who believes the government has no right to run my business or tell me what products I can sell. I can govern my own affairs. I trade on the weaknesses of others, but so does every good capitalist and every politician."

"Money can't buy you love."

"I could argue the point, but I know what you mean," Glowery said. "I buy the loyalty of my men with money and fear. That's enough. I can be a scary dude."

I nodded and stood up. "I know that," I said. "I'm plenty scared. But you can't buy me. Are we done?"

"No. I'm going to tell you what will buy you."

"Nothing I know of."

"Sure you do. Here's how it works. I keep looking for Tuco. I keep watching you. If I get my stuff back, I stop. If you destroy the stuff or Tuco's still missing in two weeks, I tell any guys I can get to ask just who did what to whom in January 1971."

"Bullshit. You don't know anything. Nobody does," I said.

"I'm not in your business, Chief. I don't need a conviction. I just need to make a threat. I'll tell them Tuco did, because I know you well enough to know you couldn't. Think about how that would go down."

"Tuco couldn't do it either."

"Well everybody says one of you had to, and my bet's on Tuco. A man in my position has to understand what people do and how they think. You couldn't do it. You're an honorable man. It's gotta be Tuco.

"You can go," he said. "Find him for me or find my stuff. You've got two weeks.

I stayed quite calm in Ghost's living room. I didn't break a sweat until I sat down in the comfort of my own car.

Rolling back down the hill to Dam road, I called Vinnie again. This time he answered and I told him he could ignore my voice mail.

CHAPTER 12

My phone rang half way down the hill. I tapped my ear piece and answered.

"Daddy, it's me," Karen said. "Mom's here. She told me about last night. Are you okay?" Her voice was shrill and strained.

"I'm fine." I said. "Just a few bruises."

"Jack's going to barbecue tonight," Karen said. "Come and stay a while."

"Your mother's there."

"She is. You come too. You'll be safe here too. It's a big house. Four bedrooms. I can find a place for anyone to sleep. Bring some friends."

"I'll come for dinner. What time?"

"With Jack on the barbecue, that's anybody's guess. Why don't you come around about four o'clock?"

"I've got group at four. If I'm fast I can probably make it a bit before 6.

"I'll tell Jack he won't have to hurry."

"See you then," I said.

I called El Cerrito P.D. They had all they wanted from my room at Floyd's house. I went back for clean clothes.

"What you running for?" Floyd asked. "We'll be ready for them this time."

"I'm the one they're after. Without me you can sleep without a gun," I said. "Karen's asked me to dinner. I'll take a room in Fremont."

I was out of his house by 2:45 and on time at the church.

Today was a different group of guys, many the same, but others different. Al lets regulars drop in and until recently we weren't growing very much. When I checked in I updated them about the assault at Floyd's house and my visit with Glowery.

"Things be heating up," said the MACSOG guy.

"Big heat," said the personnel guy from HP.

"Pointed more at Tuco than at me," I said.

"Is it only Glowery?" Al asked.

"Maybe. Maybe not. My old El Tee says somebody's asking us about a bad night 36 years ago. No one's talking."

"We've noticed," Al said.

"I don't want to talk about it."

"You could tell us. You know we wouldn't tell anyone."

"I could but I won't."

"You can trust us."

"I do trust you. You trust me. Partly you trust me because you know I know how to keep promises and secrets."

There was a little silence. We thought about promises.

"I 'state your name'?" asked MACSOG.

"Yeah," I said.

"Will support and defend the Constitution of the United States"

"And will bear true allegiance to the same."

"And follow orders"

"But only lawful orders," said Personnel.

"So help me, God," Al finished. "And he will."

"We don't all follow orders 'Shoot, shoot, shoot,' my El Tee yelled at me once. I yelled back, 'Sir, I have no target.'" Tom said.

"Only just orders," said MACSOG.

"Or not. We straightened out an asshole Lieutenant. He's alive today because he listened up," Personnel said.

"We made choices," Tom said. "Was I responsible for me or Tricky Dick? I didn't have to live with Tricky long, but I've had to live with me ever since."

"Fucking Free Fire Zones," said Personnel.

"License to Kill," said MACSOG.

I said, "Mostly lie, not license. Shoot anything that moves they said. Orders said commanders could choose without asking higher up. They didn't choose. They made us choose."

Maniacal laughter from MACSOG, "Maybe I got a license, but nobody ever issued me a fucking white tuxedo."

Usually I take the Nimitz freeway to Karen's house. Not that night. Since I was already in Lafayette, I took 680 South. Karen lives fairly close to the Fry's Electronics store just after 680 swings back over to the east side of Fremont.

When I buttoned up the Z3 I realized I had no choice but to wear my gun into the house, and I knew that Karen wouldn't like that.

I couldn't leave it in the convertible. You can't leave anything in a convertible. I learned that first time I replaced my first rag top. I don't lock the Z3 when I park it on the street. I empty the car, turn on the alarm and hope for the best.

I thought about slipping the gun into my overnight case, but I didn't know Karen's neighbors and I didn't want to make a panic. My family could live with my gun; they have for most of their lives.

Toshi answered the door in a black hakama and white kendo jacket, flushed with sweat.

Father and son had been practicing. Toshi's hair glistened and wisped about, his face the serene and athletic promise of youth. I've heard folks compare Toshi to young Tiger Woods, but that's not right. He looks like Toshiro.

He bowed as I entered. I bowed back, awkward, far too aware that I only knew this from watching Japanese movies. I'm not sure Toshi knew any better. Toshi and Jack were taught bows by an American sensei.

He gave me a hug. I caught him glancing at the bulge of my gun as we released each other.

"I don't wear this often," I said, "but there's been some trouble."

He nodded. "Grandma told us. Come on out back."

On our way we paused as Jack came down the hall. He was no longer dressed as a Samurai. His hair was damp, and he was scrubbing his neck with a towel. He tossed the towel to Toshi.

"Go change for dinner." Jack said to his son. He looked at me. "Beer?"

"Sure." Jack drinks Heineken at his house. It isn't Poleeko Gold but it's good beer.

Our women folk were in the kitchen dressed for this first hint of summer, Karen in her pink top and shorts, Lily in a sleeveless cotton dress and sandals.

Lily kissed me insistently.

"You look banged up, Daddy." Karen gave me another hug. Like Toshi, Karen eyed the bulge of my gun.

"Better me than you." I said. "You should see the other guy."

"I hate it when you say that," Karen said. "That's not the choice. Give me the gun?"

I ejected the magazine, worked the slide and verified the weapon was clear both with my eye and little finger. I handed it to her butt first, barrel pointed at the ground.

She verified it was empty with her own finger. She slipped it and the magazine into the first kitchen drawer by the slider that led out onto the patio. "So you'll know where it is," she said.

At any other home, I'd have cautioned about the child, but Toshi has been well trained. He wouldn't touch the gun. I might have worried if it was a katana instead.

"I wouldn't have brought it in but I couldn't leave it in the car."

"I understand," she said.

Jack headed through the glass slider to check the meat in the barbecue. I followed him out.

"It's a strain on her," Jack said.

"I know. It always was. She can take it if she has to."

The Tritip, darkened in the smoker, looked dry. Jack pulled a barbecue mop from his pot of secret sauce and saturated the meat, turning it over to get both sides.

"What's in that stuff?" I asked.

"Don't tell anybody," he said. "Orange juice concentrate, mustard, and ketchup with some seasoning adjustments." He took a pull on his bottle of Heineken.

"How's Lily holding up," I asked.

"Well, I'd say very clear eyed and resolute in spite of my wife." He wasn't looking at me; seemingly he was much concerned with turning the meat.

"Do you have a dog in this fight?" I asked.

"Not particularly. We don't need a gun, but frankly I don't understand why Toshi wasn't allowed to have toy ones."

I couldn't help but grin. "I remind myself that you named your son after a guy who was never a samurai but played one in movies and on T.V. Maybe it's a good idea for him not to think of guns as toys."

"Maybe."

Lily stepped out on the patio, slid her arm around me and leaned. I kissed her hair.

"How you holding up big guy?"

"Little ragged," I said. "I'm too old for this stuff."

"It's not like you volunteered."

"Our daughter may think so."

Jack mopped the meat vigorously.

At dinner the Tritip was perfect and I said so. Though smoked for hours, I was amazed how moist it was. Orange juice sealed the meat Jack said. Karen had salted and roasted new potatoes and asparagus. Toshi made the salad.

I thought Lily too effusive in her praise of Toshi's salad, but I could see that Karen was pleased, and Toshi preened as only a teenager can, basking in the attention of his two oldest and best girlfriends.

Jack smiled often at his son and wife.

I offered a toast with my beer. "Karen and Jack. Toshi. Thank you for sharing your home. To family."

"To family," they replied.

I noticed that Karen's hand did not quickly leave her glass when she set it down. Her eyes rested on her hand and glass as if still considering where to put them. My daughter was keeping thoughts to herself.

After dinner Karen served coffee in the living room. Lily asked me for the details of the night before.

"There's more to tell you about today too. I think you ought to stay here for a while."

Karen objected briefly. "I don't think Toshi has to hear this," she said.

"Let him," said Jack. "Your father won't glorify it, and Toshi needs know something about evil in the world."

So I told them what happened. I pulled no punches. I made them see the bad guy in the strongest possible light. I also let them see how helpless we were until Floyd could get his gun on the guy. I left out the reassurance that Floyd and I gave each other afterward. I didn't want to romanticize what Floyd calls the brotherhood of the blood. That would be glamorizing.

"Your friend shot this intruder twice," Karen said. "What on earth was the point of that?"

"I thought it was a good alternative to killing the poor bastard," I said. "Floyd is a crack shot. At that range he could easily kill him. Shooting him twice to disable him but not kill, Floyd gave the schmuck a chance at some kind of life though he kept on threatening ours."

"Dad, Floyd's like Boduken," Toshi said.

"Boduken?" Lily asked.

"Legendary samurai, who hated unnecessary killing." Jack replied. "He was often challenged by others trying to prove their skills. He led one to join him on an island for a duel and abandoned him stealing the boat, and said in this way he could defeat the man without lifting a hand."

"I wouldn't say Floyd was quite that good," I said.

Karen was looking at her lap. I hoped she was pleased with Toshi's insight, but somehow I doubted it.

"I've got more updates, and I'm afraid they don't bode well. Somebody is out to get Tuco. And maybe if I'm not careful will come after me too." I told them about the morning's conversation with Glowery and finally summed up.

"Tuco took something from Glowery. He wants it back and he wants Tuco. He figures he can get both if he's following me."

"I can see why you want me out of the way," Lily said.

"I didn't know half of this when I called last night. I think you ought to stay here for at least a few days."

"Mom can stay as long as she wants."

"Thank you, dear."

"You're welcome. You stay too, Daddy. You'll be safe here."

"Thanks but no thanks. I'm pretty safe already. Glowery's counting on me to find Tuco for him."

Karen's lower lip began to quiver. "I hate it when you suddenly go out at night with a gun. I've hated it all my life." She began to cry.

I glanced at Toshi. To my mind the pain of his mother was another truth he needed to understand.

Karen continued. "Anytime you got called after midnight, I could never sleep. After a while I found out that Mom wasn't sleeping either."

"True, but I always made you promise never to tell." Lily said. Her eyes were glistening now.

"She never did until now," I said.

"And would not have yet," said Lily. "You needed to be a peace keeper."

I went to Karen, leaned over her chair and cradled her head against my chest. "In any family, someone must always face the darkness, daughter. Don't cry for me. Maybe cry for Tuco. Lucky for us, we've done this before, and I hope you never have to."

"I know you always look after him," she cried. "But why? Uncle Tuco's not even our blood."

I laughed and knelt down beside her where I could look her in the eye. "Do you hear yourself my proud black daughter? You are the daughter of my heart, but the blood daughter of Owen Albright. That's your Irish birth Mom over there. I'm something European, Celtic and maybe Semitic. Tuco's not your blood or mine, but neither am I. Family is the cherished refuge we choose to honor, and not just something compelled by accident of birth."

I poured myself another cup of decaf and busied myself with the cream.

"Mom says Tuco doesn't want you to follow him."

"Probably to protect me, and maybe at the beginning to protect his friend Newton.

"I don't know what they stole from Glowery. I don't think it was drugs. The drug market's here. There's a surplus in Mexico, and I don't think Tuco would worry too much about drugs if that was the load. Whatever it was is bound to be pretty illegal. If Newton was doing something illegal, Tuco would only be jamming him up further to involve me. And Tuco was taking a big chance in Glowery's back yard. I know that doesn't scare him.

"Maybe he thinks there's nothing I can do. Maybe he thinks he'd just be putting me at risk if he dragged me into it. Maybe, maybe, maybe. It doesn't matter. Like it or not, I'm in it now. I've got his back just as he has always had mine."

Karen stared at Toshi for minute. She seemed to want him to look at her. She wanted him to do something. Whatever it was she wasn't going to say it. Toshi seemed oblivious to her. His eyes were fixed on me.

I smiled, hoping to be reassuring.

"Daddy, what was the bad thing that Tuco did in the war?"

"That's not quite what I'd call it, Karen. Everything about war is bad. You're forced into decisions you wish no one has to make. Sometimes you have to do something painful."

"Tell me. Tell me and Toshi."

"Well..." I'd told this story in group. I had repeated it to Al Starr only days before, but I had never told my family. I made them wait quite a while.

"Here goes, as short as possible. Tuco caught the duty as gate guard at Phouc Vinh. A company was coming in. Civilian workers crowded the gate. Suddenly Tuco saw a toddler wandering toward the company of grunts. What he's carrying looks like a toy ball, but it isn't. It's a grenade and the pin's out.

"Tuco yelled a lot, but no one heard him, or heard but couldn't listen. What was he supposed to do? Let the kid walk in and blow up grunts? Blow away the kid?

"He says he tried to shoot the grenade out of the baby's hand. I believe him. If it worked he'd feel all right, but of course it made no difference when the grenade went off."

"Tuco has told me the story more than once," Lily said. "I always tell him he didn't kill that child. The killer pulled the pin."

Karen bit her lower lip. "Were you there, Daddy?"

"No, but I was another time when more than a hundred Montagnard tribesmen were walking toward our ambush. Were they driven by NVA or just walking down the road? We had new guys on the machine guns. They were nervous as cats. We were in a free fire zone. Anyone could pull the trigger. What to do? I was a squad leader. I kept looking to the El Tee, but he didn't know either."

"What happened?"

"Tuco stepped out on the trail with his weapon pointed at them and yelled. If the enemy was there, they'd have killed him."

"What if he hadn't stepped out?"

"I don't think I'd be here. I'd maybe be in a loony bin somewhere. Imagine a hundred innocents killed with only our guns firing. Can you imagine the horror? All of us might have been court marshaled. Maybe it'd be worse to have the nightmares. Today I might be dead, or maybe dead drunk. I'd rather be dead than live with the consequences of that slaughter. Tuco knew the choice and made it more quickly than anyone else could."

Toshi's mouth was hanging open.

"Toshiro it is not always like that. I never had to make choices quite like either of these. I hope you never have to. On the whole it might be better to be like your samurai and always find an alternative. On the other hand if you have to make a choice, I know you, and I know you'll make a good one."

"You're making one now," Lily said. "Do what you have to. Be careful, be well, and be safe. Find our friend and keep him from harm."

I checked into the Fremont Hilton for the night. Maybe I paid more than I needed to, but I was tired and didn't want to search around.

Still I didn't sleep. I kept thinking about the trails I was following and what signs I had for them. Something was missing and it made me itch.

First of all I had bad guys on my trail; maybe one would trip and let me know who the real bad guys were. I was tracing down Tuco's last case. I didn't know what I'd learn, but maybe something. I didn't have too much faith in my missing person's report. If Tuco was hiding from Glowery and maybe from me, he was surely well hid from cops. There was only one thing left now, the itch I couldn't scratch, at least alone, but maybe I knew where to get help.

I hadn't cleared my cell phone logs. I found the 414 number and pushed the send key.

"Bookman," he said.

"It's me, Blondie" I said.

"How you doing, Sarge? What's up?"

"Are you awake?"

"I'm a night owl, Blondie. I wasn't asleep. Don't worry about it. Still the best of friends."

"Hardly that," I said, "but let me take you off the wild goose chase. I know why Tuco's running now, and who he's running from."

I told him about Newton and Glowery. "Tuco's hiding from Ghost, I said. "Ghost's trying to survive in a tough business. I don't think Tuco will have to wait long."

"Ghost, huh? I'm not surprised. I had to get tough with him once or twice. He was hard to control."

"It's my guess; Ghost doesn't feel fear like you and me."

"Must be nice," the El Tee said. "But Ghost's not Tuco's only problem. I talked to Skeeter this afternoon. A guy from the CID came to see him with a lot questions."

"What did he do?"

"Told the guy to go to hell, get a warrant or get a subpoena," the El Tee said.

"You'd think they'd talk to me," I said. "After all I was an officer of the law and something of a public personality."

"Unless you're the prime suspect," he said.

That shut me up for a bit.

"Look I don't know how you fix this," the El Tee said. "I think you've got to find him and figure this out. If one of you gets accused maybe the only way out is to blame the other."

"I don't know," I said. "After this much time it might feel better to confess."

"You should know."

"Well I'm not accusing or confessing," I said. "I'm going to find him and we'll see. I've got to find him anyway to take Ghost off his back."

"And how will you do that?"

"I'll get Tuco to tell me where Ghost's stuff is and make a trade. Ghost can have his stuff, if he leaves me and Tuco alone."

The El Tee chuckled. "It's quite a problem. Damned if you do and damned if you don't. I don't think you can do a good deed by giving a gangster what he wants. You know damn well that one way or another giving in to him is going to hurt somebody else."

I thought about Tuco's baby problem on the Phouc Vinh gate.

"I guess we'll keep on keeping on," the El Tee said. "Sometimes the only way out is through."

"I've heard that a lot lately," I said, "and I've said it to myself."

"I'll keep tracking on the CID thing," he said. "You look for Tuco. Keep me informed and let me know if I can help."

"Okay."

"Goodbye for now," he said. "I've got to get some sleep."

I miss Lily at night. Sleeping in a strange bed makes it worse.

I learned a trick in the Army that helps. Whenever I was on watch, I noticed that I dozed off more often if I was trying too hard to be awake.

Now when sleep doesn't come, I focus my eyes on some shadow in the dark that I can't quite see. This is easier now that I wear glasses, and easier still as my corrections grow worse. I study the shadow and try to make firm shape of it, all the while keeping my eyes open and trying not to blink until eventually my eyes grow heavy and sleep finally steals the will to try.

CHAPTER 13

The next morning was Friday. My appointment at the Foxhole to ask about Tuco and Newton was for 10:30. Breakfast at the hotel would have been convenient but too expensive. Foxhole is in Richmond, next door to El Sobrante. I was much further south in Fremont but for me, way south. The stop and go traffic of the morning commute on the freeway was in my way.

I took Mission Boulevard instead. The speed was about the same with the traffic lights in Hayward, but from Hayward I caught Redwood Road in Castro Valley. Eventually it crosses Skyline Boulevard on the crest of the hills in Oakland, and drops from Skyline down to Highway 13. It would have been a slow drive in a sedan, but in the Z3 it was morning recreation.

I had noticed a Chevy Silverado several times well behind me on Mission. I didn't see him on Redwood, but at Skyline, I turned south instead, looped around and parked on the East side of Skyline well back from Redwood among other cars.

The Silverado was only five minutes behind me. Not bad for a pickup on a country road.

Ghost's guy was talking on his cell phone and headed down the hill to 13. I watched him roll out of sight and then continued north on Skyline to 24 and then East to Camino Pablo. Camino Pablo is the fancy name they give to Dam Road in fancy Lafayette. Shortly I was sitting back at the counter in El Soleil with time enough for breakfast.

Hodiak showed up for his breakfast too, eating at the other end of the counter. I decided not to notice. He couldn't tail me himself, but I could leave him the illusion that he hadn't been spotted so he could if he wished assign someone else.

After breakfast I headed for San Pablo Avenue and turned south. Long ago San Pablo Avenue was the main highway, when there were few zoning requirements. In Richmond San Pablo is lined on both sides with old burger joints, bar and grills, used car dealerships, mechanics, tire stores, old strip malls and, where traffic justified, newer developments with the big franchise grocery stores.

Foxhole's storefront has looked the same for years. Indeed even in that neighborhood Foxhole begins to look a little seedy. San Pablo has upgraded a little over time, but Foxhole has not. Everything was painted black, maybe to hide dirt, or maybe somebody gave them free black paint and they found enough volunteers.

The interior was one large room divided into offices by eight foot mobile partitions. I was just in time so a veteran volunteer escorted me to the conference space. The staff was seated in a circle in an odd lot of chairs that had never been seen in an office supply store. The vacant seat was a ragged love seat which had apparently been saved just for me.

Gary Workman, balding, corduroy slacks and blue workshirt introduced himself and then his senior staff: Sheila Green, long skirt, blouse, and former blond but now dyed green, (and I had thought that out of style); Ron Ellis, tall black man elegantly dressed in long sleeved silk shirt, black jeans, and highly polished boots; and finally retired CSM Peter Rudin, sized for an NFL lineman too old to play but with shoulder length white hair.

I commented on the hair.

"Couldn't grow it out while I was in the Army," Rudin said. "Thought I'd give it a try now that I'm out."

I looked to Workman. "Is this everyone?" I asked. "I can see there's a lot more seats."

"This is all the staff here today. We have the volunteers in at 11:30 when we're finished. Few of them knew Newton. Some would know Tuco, but not in this context. You've now met everyone who is important.

"I've told you all something of Mr. Duvall's business, but I'll let him explain it."

"Thank you, Gary," I said. "I'll introduce myself again. I'm George Duvall. If you've been here a while, you've heard my name before. Before I retired I was the Chief of Police for El Sobrante. I'm not here in that capacity this morning. I am here as a concerned friend and colleague of Tuco Ruis."

"I believe you already know that Tuco's disappeared. I told Gary the other day. I've learned more since we spoke. The late Keith Newton is involved. Perhaps you know he was at least briefly tangled up with the notorious Richard Glowery who lives in El Sobrante.

"For the record my department was very aware of Mr. Glowery and his local activities. In El Sobrante. He never gave us a reason to arrest him, until, arguably, yesterday when he briefly may have threatened me with an illegal firearm.

"Also for the record, improbable though it seems, Glowery, Tuco, and I all served in the same 1st Cav Recon platoon a long time ago. Tuco had another run in with Glowery after we all came home. I'm telling you this because it may help to explain Tuco's motivations."

I told them about my conversation with Glowery the day before and the conclusions I had already reached. I didn't tell them Glowery was having me followed.

"The other day when I called Gary, I knew that Tuco had pulled Newton out of some trap, but not what kind. I know now, but I don't know why.

"Tuco told me he was going after Newton for Ms. Theresa Garcia. He told Ms. Garcia he wanted her to pretend to be my client because he didn't think you guys would do it. I'm wondering what he told you, and I'm wondering if there was another dodge.

"I don't know what Tuco and Newton took from Glowery. I don't know how or why Newton got mixed up with Glowery, or how and why Tuco got mixed up in it with Newton. I am hoping you can tell me."

Sheila Green said, "I'm going to be real straight with you. It doesn't help that you're a cop."

"Try not to let it bother you," I said.

"Sometimes our clients are rousted by cops," she said.

"My wife would tell you I call myself a peace officer. I don't think I'm the kind of cop that worries you. Oh I've busted vets when I had to, but like as not most of the time my desk sergeant gave you guys a call."

"I've got some of those calls," Rudin said.

"Me too," said Green reluctantly. "But if you're a friend to vets why haven't we seen you down here before?"

"Because I'm a cop. Because I would make your clients a little nervous. You catch guys on the bad end here. You look after the drunks, the homeless, the guys whose old lady just kicked them out of the house. I look like the enemy to them and they don't sit quite right with me either."

"Tuco told us he was going with you to group in Lafayette," Green said.

"Yeah."

"And why not here?"

"I think it's a different problem," I said. "The guys in Lafayette look squared away. They're wearing button down shirts and shiny loafers every day. They're hardly down and out. What problem could they be thought to have compared to what your guys are up against? I don't know that your guys have got more pain, but your guys' pains are obvious. For the guys in Lafayette, me included, we're there in part because nobody else believes in how we hurt."

Green nodded. "My beef isn't just with you, but with boss man over there." She nodded toward Workman. "He gave you a list of our clients without thinking much about your privacy."

"Don't worry about it," I said. "I haven't talked to anybody on that list, and I won't. After my visit with Glowery, I don't think I have to. I already know where Tuco and Newton ended up.

"Maybe it would help if you thought of me as another veteran client," I said.

THE LAST LOST WARRIOR

"Tuco and I sometimes argue, but we're the best of friends. Each of us owes the other his life. I can't just leave him swinging in the wind."

"But apparently he wants to swing. I thought you said he doesn't want your help," Rudin said.

"I also said it was because he didn't want to put me at risk. That ought to be my choice, not his. And I'm damn sure he knows what I would choose. I've risked my butt for him countless times as he has done for me. There's no stopping that."

I let them chew on that for a while, then said, "I'm not exactly a combat virgin and neither is Tuco, but I've probably had more experience with guys like Glowery than he ever will. I've been going up against bad guys on the job all my life. This time it's not the job. This time it's Tuco."

"Tuco told me how he took on Glowery that first time," Workman said.

"He did. A good job too, but he had me outside as back up."

Green still looked skeptical. Ellis and Workman were relaxed. Rudin stared at a high window above Workman's desk. His eyes were moist.

"Leave no man behind," he said. Ellis and Green looked at each other. Green nodded.

"Exactly," I said. Rudin smiled and I knew he understood.

"I knew Newton's father," Rudin said. "I served with him. He was a World War II Army vet. Joined the Pennsylvania National Guard afterward and got activated for Korea. Big war hero in Korea. Got a direct commission as an officer and retired as a Brigadier General after a long distinguished career.

"Newton was never going to live up to that, but he thought he had to. He joined the Marines instead of the Army, but it probably made no difference. By now you learned enough to know his life was a mess. Everything he touched had turned to shit.

"A month or two ago, Keith came to see me. He looked a new man, bright eyed and bushy tailed as we used to say. He was here to tell me all about it. He had a new job. He was back in the combat saddle again, riding shotgun for a trucking company.

"I told him I thought that was pretty strange. I didn't think there were a lot of trucks with goods so valuable in them that the trucker wouldn't reasonably be his own security. Keith said he didn't know what was in the trucks, but he didn't have to know. He was getting paid to carry a gun again, and his boss, a Mr. Claude Hodiak thought he was something special.

"I live in El Sobrante too," Rudin said. "I live close enough to Glowery's compound to know who Hodiak was. I told Newton that I knew Hodiak worked for Glowery. Newton said he had met Mr. Glowery and Mr. Glowery liked him too.

"I told him, I thought he was playing with fire."

"The next bit's mine," Green said. "We had all talked about Newton's dangerous new profession. Tuco had stopped in for coffee one morning. I knew they had been close. I told him about it. He seemed shocked. He asked where Keith was working. None of us knew. He immediately asked for a meeting with staff and Newton's friends. We brainstormed. I made up the list of friends who might know. He told me 'Sheila if he comes in, tell him I'm looking for him.' and that was the last I saw of Tuco until we learned Keith was killed."

"Let's see if I've got this straight. Sergeant Major, you knew Newton was in trouble, but you didn't do anything about it at first?"

"No," he said. "I couldn't imagine what I could do."

"But you all told Tuco and he appealed to you for help."

"That's about it," Workman said. "He asked. We helped."

I suppose I got quiet for a while. I scratched my head, pulled at my jaw and looked at the floor.

"What's bugging you?" Ellis asked.

"My own ignorance, I guess. Tuco worked this overtime. He worked me; he worked Garcia, and worked all of you. What's he working for? He put himself in the gun sight of one of the most dangerous men in the county, Richard Glowery, a guy I knew in the Nam as Ghost.

"I guess we know Tuco was doing it for Newton, but who was Newton that he meant so much? What's the connection?" I asked them. "Tuco said that Keith was his oldest friend except for me. What got them together?"

"I've been here longer than anybody," Gary said," and I don't know. Anybody else?"

Ellis and Rudin shook their heads. Sheila Green shrugged her shoulders.

"If you like I'll call some of the staff who moved on," Gary said. "Meanwhile what we do know is that Tuco went after him. He was back here within a week. Tuco said Newton was on an island, and did we know anybody who had a boat?"

"Did you?"

"No. But a week later Tuco and Keith were back here together and we learned that Keith had quit Hodiak and Glowery."

"Keith looked great," Rudin said. "I was quite upset when I heard he was killed. Of course it was Glowery, but no one will ever prove it."

"And how did you find that out?" I asked.

"Tuco told us."

Tuco had his hand in everything. For all I knew Newton had gotten himself mixed up with Glowery because Tuco told him about his old run in. He had recruited the Foxhole staff to find Newton and recruited Teri Garcia to officially hire me.

I thanked them for their time, went back to the cottage, made myself a grilled ham and cheese sandwich for lunch, and sat down with a yellow legal pad of paper.

I drew up a time line of events. Since Glowery was involved, I went all the way back to Tuco's first encounter with him.

I tried to make a list of "clues" I could still act on. Yearning's email was first on the list, but I was still reluctant to write to her. I was afraid it might come off as, "Dear Yearning, I have invaded your privacy, exposed your love life, and now want you to betray your new boyfriend." I had to think of something better to say.

The key from under the desk did me no good at all without the matching padlock, but there was something there, an itch in the back of my mind that I couldn't scratch. There was no sense worrying about it. Eventually it would occur to me. I folded up the envelope with the key inside and stuck it in my wallet.

I put down the pad and made myself a cup of tea. Floyd had some plastic chairs out in the yard; I put one of them in the sunshine, sat down, sipped my tea, and tried to think about Tuco, not as a case but as a person. I had a little conversation with myself; talk I couldn't share with anyone.

Perhaps others won't think so, but I think of Tuco as a very moral person.

Generally he's responsible for his choices and committed to them because of his values. Even the bad stuff in the bush those long years ago was a carefully thought out moral choice; he meant to protect our platoon. Never mind he turned out to be wrong. That was a Tuco I understood; that was the Tuco that warned the folks in his marijuana operation that Glowery was taking over. Tuco used me for backup, but kept me out of risk.

And there's the rub. Why would he mire himself in the chaos and insanity of a biker drug gang again? These men were dangerous - mad some of them - and quite unpredictable. He extracted himself from the crooked life years ago only now to plunge back in. I couldn't figure that out.

Tuco and Newton had done something extraordinary. They stole a van with something contraband from a drug lord. They stole it from his well protected property, and he didn't know how they stole it.

At the moment I didn't give a damn about how. I could find that out with some work. What I couldn't get was why.

Newton sounded very much like a lost soul, aimless but for some memory of the soldier he'd been. Tuco would have known him for who he was. Newton was probably doomed before Tuco joined him on that island, and if he was doomed what was the point of rescuing him?

Maybe I had to find the van to find that out.

CHAPTER 14

I spent Friday afternoon on the telephone. Cops watched Glowery's island as best they could. I hoped to hook up with their surveillance and get some idea of what I was up against. Unfortunately Glowery's island isn't in Contra Costa or Alameda County where I know lots of cops. Glowery's island was in San Joaquin. On the telephone I was looking for somebody who might know somebody who might be able to help.

Bob Schooner, working undercover, knew cops in every adjacent county. He put me in touch with a Captain Arsenal in the San Joaquin County Sheriff's Department. My badge number was verified; I was sworn to secrecy. After a while I got a telephone call from a man named Chuck Wang. We talked for quite a while.

Chuck's dad sold Glowery most of the island, leaving only the old Wang place with its dock. Chuck lived there now and mostly kept out of the gang's business, except to keep Arsenal informed about general movements.

With Chuck Wang's help maybe I could investigate this missing van from a safe distance.

I slept in Floyd's cottage on Friday night but I left at five in the morning to drive through the Delta. Highway 160 leaves Highway 4 at Pittsburg. 160 rides the top of a levee so you see farms on your right and river on your left. I got breakfast at a greasy spoon in Rio Vista, and took Highway 12 across the farmland below the levee and followed another levee to the Ox Bow Marina.   By 7 a.m. I was standing on the temporary mooring dock near the store.

I wore blue-denim bib overalls, gum boots, and a broad straw hat with a turkey feather stuck in the band. These are my gardening clothes. I like sun off my face and I want to wear something that I don't have to protect from the dirt while I'm mucking about.   You don't see a lot of bib overalls anymore. I was confident in my costume. Chuck had a very clear idea of how I'd look.

An aluminum skiff approached the dock.   There was an empty back rest on the bow of the boat. The only other seat was in the stern. The middle of the boat was taken with a large, boxy livewell. The guy at the tiller killed the engine and dropped some fenders over the side. He didn't look a thing like me. He was a Chinese American man wearing khaki pants, a plaid shirt, an orange life vest, and a billed cap with a World Series of Poker logo. He didn't get out of the boat, but looked up at me and called out, "Mr. Duckworth?"

We'd agreed on this signal. I didn't want him yelling my real name at a public dock. I climbed aboard and shook his hand.

"Chuck Wang," he said quietly. "Pleased to meet you Chief Duvall. Put this on."

I was soon encased in my own orange life vest.

He restarted the motor, and moved out into the channel at a slow speed.

"This is a 70 horse motor," Chuck said. "Once I crank it up we can only talk to each other by shouting, so let's get some details out of the way first. Can you cast with a spinning reel?"

"Not for a long time," I said, "but I'll manage."

"You probably won't have to," Chuck said. "I got out early this morning and caught a couple of bass. They're in the well. You can net one and show it off if anyone asks us how we're doing. Most of bass fishing is about running about looking for likely spots to fish. If we're moving, that's what people will assume we're doing. I hope you never have to pick up a pole.

"Here's the plan. I'm going to gun down the channel for a while, then we'll have to take it slow. There's a couple of islands nestled up near mine and the channels are narrow. If we speed through there we'd piss off the locals slopping the boats against their docks and scaring the fish. Going slow we'll be able to talk, but quietly. Sound carries better over water. I'm going talk kind of folksy and maybe even tell a few jokes. We need generally to sound as if we're a couple guys out here having fun. Okay?"

I nodded.

As soon as we got to the main channel, Chuck turned up the throttle. He was right. It was too loud, not only the engine, but also the wind in the open boat and the rhythmic slap of the aluminum hull against the wind driven chop. I didn't bother to shout, but tried to look around.

The Delta from the river seems primitive compared to the view from the road. There are no towns. The levee rises high above the sides of the channel, broken only by other channels, inlets, sloughs, and islands. Sometimes there's a house on the spine of a levee. Island homes are rare.

Arsenal told me that Chuck Wang's family had lived on their island home for generations. Some of Chuck's ancestors came to California to build a railroad for Huntington, Hopkins, Stanford, and Crocker. When that was done they built the Delta levees and drained the delta for farms. A few of Chuck's family stayed and lived for a while by fishing the river. A sturdy house was built on stilts on a rock that anchored Wang Island. When it washed away twice by flood the family built it again. The third house, the current one, was raised on girders of steel.

Chuck said his father had practiced law in Sacramento. For his father the house on the river was only a summer retreat. The old man sold most of the island to a man he thought was a developer. He hoped more homes would increase the value of his older place. On his next visit he discovered his mistake. His island house was surrounded by barbed wire, locking him in.

"Wang doesn't want to leave," Arsenal told me. "And he won't let Glowery drive him out."

Chuck never complained that his father sold him out, but he became San Joaquin County's eyes and ears on "Glowery's" island. "We don't have to pay him," said the Captain at the Sheriff's Department. "He does it for love."

It didn't look like love from the bow of the boat, but maybe there's something laconic about all outdoors-men when they are about their business. His hand on the tiller was very steady despite the chop, but he seemed completely relaxed as if he was indeed a simple fishing guide about his business.

Glancing over my shoulder I could see that here the channel split. I twisted around to look at the seeming mass of land between them. Wang cut down the throttle. As we approached I could see the smaller, narrow channels between the islands, so narrow in some places that tree limbs met overhead.

Wang turned the boat into one of the wider openings. After only a few yards the channel opened again. We seemed suddenly to be in a small lake, though there was a clear current. I knew we were surrounded by islands; I'd looked at this bay on the chart the day before. Here in our low boat the channels were all but invisible, concealed by tall reeds but suddenly revealed as our boat drew up.

Wang threaded the boat through one of these and after a few turns announced, "Here we are."

The first floor of each house was at least ten feet in the air and reached by stairs. We were gliding in front of the homes. Now I faced forward on the bow seat, the morning sun was on my right. These homes sat on the eastern edge of the island well sheltered by trees.

"Up ahead on the left is the house you want to look at," Chuck said. "The fourth one in. The van was parked under the house."

"There's no dock," I said.

There was a gentle slope from beneath the house to the edge of the water. One could beach a skiff there, but I couldn't imagine how you could beach a hull with enough displacement to move a loaded van.

"Correct. It looks as if they must have used another dock to take it out. Hodiak asked me about that. He thought maybe the guys used my dock."

"Sure," I said. "They drove over here and silently took down the barbwire fence, drove through onto your dock and with rubber hammers put the fence back again."

"I told him I'd another reason to know they hadn't used my dock. I showed him how I knew. My dock is alarmed. Nothing fancy. It just rings a buzzer in my house if someone steps on it.

"Hodiak didn't like that."

Tossing fenders over the side, Wang pulled the skiff up alongside his dock. We clambered out. I tried to keep my hat pulled down. It wasn't likely there was anyone out here who could recognize me, but why take a chance.

Chuck Wang made good coffee. I stood well back from his windows and tried to check out the area where the van had been with a good pair of binoculars.

"There are some tire tracks near the water's edge," I said.

"That's how they brought it on," Chuck said. "They put a ramp down from the side of their ferry and drove it under the house. You could tell the van was well loaded. The ground is soft and the tracks are deep."

I'd have liked a closer look, but I could hardly do that without being closely observed by someone along the row.

"Newton showed up with the truck?"

"From what you told me it was him. Tall man, jar head haircut. Seemed like he was always carrying some kind of gun."

A telephone rang, Wang's cell, ring tone set as an old fashioned phone.

"Yeah, I got a client. Name of Duckworth.

"Uh huh. You don't say.

"Well I guess I can have anybody I want at my house.

"He wants to talk to you," he said handing me the telephone.

"If you wanted to look around the island, Duvall" said Hodiak in my ear," all you had to do was ask."

"I didn't think your boss would like it much. After he waved around that shotgun I didn't want to take a chance."

"I ain't Glowery and he ain't here. I'm in charge. Why don't you meet me at the end of Wang's dock? Where are you parked?"

"Horseshoe Marina."

"I can run you back when you're done. Tell Wang to go fish."

"Let me use the can and I'll be right out," I said.

I called Arsenal on my cell. "Captain this is George Duvall. Claude Hodiak has just invited me to poke around Glowery's island. If I haven't called you by tomorrow morning, you ought to be able to get your search warrant."

I'm not prejudiced but maybe I suffer from cultural stereotyping. Wang's grin seemed too big for his face.

Hodiak had a big shallow draft cabin cruiser maybe 26 feet long. He hadn't bothered to tie up, but held his boat against the dock with a loop of rope thrown around a cleat. I stepped aboard; he flipped off the loop, and backed the boat. The channel in front of Wang's dock was only about twenty feet wide, too narrow for him to easily turn the boat around.

"I get it," Hodiak said. "Ruis and Newton stole something here. If you find the something maybe you find Ruis."

"Or maybe I give it back and get your boss off of Tuco's back."

"I'll bet," Hodiak said doubtfully.

We pulled into another dock.

"This is my place," Hodiak said. "Glowery rarely comes here anymore. He seems to prefer that cat house of his in El Sobrante. I think it's the white rugs."

He dropped some fenders fore and aft and tied up the boat.

"Come on up. I ain't inviting you into my place, but that doesn't interest you much anyway. Let's take a walk."

We crossed the frontage of a house. A bearded face leaned over the balcony.

"It's okay Claw. I'm just showing this guy around."

Claw nodded and the face disappeared.

"Here it is, Glowery's place where the dirt was done."

"This was Glowery's personal place?"

"And his personal deal, personal Econoline van, and personal guard. All his personal business. This is where the van was parked."

"Nose in?"

"Yeah."

Claude was being pretty loose and in a rebellious mood. I took a chance. "What was in the van." I asked.

"I've got no damned idea," Hodiak said. "I don't want to know. I didn't look. None of my business. It's Glowery's retirement plan, some deal he made with our partners in Mexico. He's got a place down there on the Baja coast. He figured to deliver this load, collect some big pay, retire, and wait for dusty death. Says he wants to die with his dick in the mouth of a sweet Mexican whore. Just between you and me I don't think he gets it up any other way these days."

"And you get nothing, Hodiak? You've got no interest at all."

"Oh I've got interest all right. I get the brass ring. I inherit this whole outfit. Quite a jump from where I came from. I was just a runaway kid when Glowery picked me up, and now I run the whole business, but nobody's noticed.

"This was the deal. I manage some security for the truck. He stashes it on the island while he's setting things up. Then he drives for the border and never comes back. I don't say anything. I just keep running the show. Eventually everybody figures out that I'm in charge. No big deal. He just drives down and disappears."

"He was going to drive?"

"He or the soldier boys, Newton and Ruis, but not now."

"And afterward?"

"Not my problem," Hodiak said. "If you want my opinion, I think maybe the two of them disappear too."

But probably not into retirement, I thought. Glowery'd kill them if the Mexican mob didn't. Tuco would've known, and maybe Newton guessed. Or maybe he wouldn't want to guess or even care; suicide by thug would work as well as suicide by cop. Glowery's load would be a good way to do it. He could go out in one last gun down. Wouldn't matter who did it, Glowery, cops, or other gangsters. Wouldn't matter, he'd be going down with a gun in hand, apparently the only way he was really happy in the world.

I knew a guy like that in Vietnam. The guys said he was addicted to combat and always taking a chance. Once he stayed behind alone and called in an air strike on his own position. We called him Ghost.

I was looking around the slope below the house.

"So when did Tuco show up?" I asked.

"Just a few weeks after Newton moved in. Newton cleared it with Glowery. He said Tuco was an old war buddy and maybe they could take Tuco along for the ride."

"Did Newton tell him Tuco's name?"

"Glowery knew. He didn't care. He figured Tuco knew how to handle himself."

I grinned. "I guess we've got some proof of that."

"Glowery came out fine last time," Hodiak said. "It wasn't Glowery that got clubbed in the head."

"So he let him party instead."

"Wasn't much. There are always women on the island. I don't remember that it was especially their party. It was just Saturday night, and Glowery happened to be here."

"When guys would get stoned or distracted."

"Don't you tell him I said so, but Glowery was out of it."

The tire tracks told a clear story to me. The tracks were several weeks old now, faded, and washed a bit by rain, but the soil was a thick, clay mud, the tires new. The story was clear to me. The van had backed down the slope, tires turned to the left, backed up the slope, turned left and forward again toward the water.

"Looks like it was loaded on a boat."

"Duh," said Hodiak. "How else could they get it off?"

He wasn't fooling me. He'd ignored the tracks, didn't try, or couldn't read them. He'd accused Chuck Wang of lending the thieves his dock.

"There was always another possibility," I said. "Half of this island is a jungle. They might have just hid it. Since they didn't, we're looking for a boat, something special, big enough to carry a loaded van, small enough to get through your channel, and quiet enough not to wake anybody up. Wasn't your company boat huh? I imagine you checked."

"Nah. It was locked up on its usual berth at Horseshoe."

"So I'm looking for another special boat."

"Good luck," Hodiak said. "I hope you find it. I hope you find your friend.

"But don't screw up. You're still a cop. You'd still like to see Glowery put away. Don't mess about. No tricks."

"What do you mean?"

"Find the damned van and give it back. Let Glowery get away clean. If he gets stuck or taken down, I'll be dead meat too. This mob's a wolf pack, and I'm only the number two wolf. If you suck him down some guys will figure me for a candy ass. I won't stay head wolf; they'll just kill me. If somehow I survive you watch your ass 'cause I'll be after you. I've worked this for more than twenty five years but most of it's off the books. I won't even get decent Social Security. If Glowery goes down too soon, I'll have nothing left."

I told him I'd keep that in mind. He had me back to the marina by one o'clock. I was back at the cottage by three.

CHAPTER 15

Next morning the El Tee called. "How's the hunt?"

I told him about my visit to the island. "I think it would take some special kind of boat to load and carry a heavy van. Maybe that will give me a way to trace it."

"Maybe I've got some intel on my end," the El Tee said. "I think the CID isn't exactly the CID"

"No it's not exactly," I said. "The letters used to stand for Criminal Investigative Division. Now it's called the Criminal Investigative Command but they kept the old initials."

"That's not what I meant."

"What did you mean?"

"There's just one guy. He's got credentials, but I think there's just one of them. I talked to Rock yesterday. The guy had been to see him. His description sounded like Skeeter's, so I got them to talk to each other. Skeeter lives in Michigan and Rock lives in South Carolina. Both of them were interviewed by a guy who is missing the tip of his left pinky finger."

"So?"

"So that's not how they do things," the El Tee said. "In an ordinary investigation there's a case manager somewhere, but if witnesses are scattered around the country they get interviewed by local guys. The reports go back to the manager."

"But he's got credentials."

"So he does," the El Tee said. "He's CID but he's probably not on a priority mission or an officially active one. This is a very old case. Why should it be important now? It's probably not an active case. Maybe Pinky Finger makes old cases a hobby. Maybe the Army's nervous, but doesn't want to look into it officially so he's doing it privately."

"Doesn't it make it official if he flashes credentials?"

"I don't think so, but what does it matter? Official or not he's asking questions. You can bet if he gets answers he'll make it official. You've got to get in front of this, Blondie."

How was I supposed to do that?

"Maybe I shouldn't give a damn," the El Tee said. "It's your problem, not mine. I need my security clearance for work, but it's past time to retire anyway. I'm not going to be accused of murder."

That was certainly the old El Tee that I knew. If Tuco or me went down we must have screwed up somehow and it wouldn't be his fault.

I got off the telephone as quickly as I could and went to work on the problem of the boat.

The minimum cargo capacity had to be the weight of a Ford Econoline Van with cargo. With maximum payload, according to Edmonds.com, was about 12,000 pounds. Was Glowery's van fully loaded? The depth of the tire tracks suggested it was close.

According to Chuck Wang the channel around the island was mostly about eight feet deep, but there were a couple of spots where it was only five. The channel in front of his dock was only fifteen feet wide, probably the narrowest passage. A large vessel could easily maneuver in the lake like bay in front of Glowery's "cabin" but it would still have to squeeze past Chuck Wang's dock.

I was therefore looking for a boat with fifteen feet of beam or less with a draft of no more than four feet but still with the cargo capacity of more than 12,000 pounds.

This is a description that fits many boats, but not too many in the San Joaquin Delta. Stockton and Sacramento both have deep water ports, on the San Joaquin and Sacramento rivers respectively. The shipping channels are deep. The Port of Sacramento's channel is kept dredged to 30 feet. Freight moves on the river but usually in much larger craft.

Some of the larger pleasure craft would be big enough to carry the van, but they weren't equipped with a cargo ramp or a heavy hoist. The tire tracks made me think they used a ramp.

I started my inquiries with the staff at the Ports. No go.

"This is a deep water port, young man," said an officious voice from Port of Sacramento. Why would we bother with boats so small?"

"I'd talk to the marinas," said the operations manager at the Port of Stockton. "There are some amazing boats on the Delta. One time I saw a Chinese junk... or at least a close facsimile."

I made a list of marinas. After consulting Google maps, I put them in order of proximity to the island and started making calls, many calls.

During a pause, Floyd telephoned me. "How about lunch?" We went to Barclays on College Avenue, ate flat iron steaks and puzzled over which beer to drink next.

I told Floyd about my frustrating search. "I started first thing this morning. I thought it would be easy. That boat's got to be pretty unique. It ought to stand out in the crowd and catch a waterman's eye the way a blond with gloves to her elbows catches mine."

"Maybe," Floyd said. "Or maybe it stands out, but they never think of it carrying a car."

"Well I've left my phone number all over the Delta. Maybe I'll get lucky."

Floyd laughed. "We both know Tuco's a sharp guy. Doesn't care too much about the rules. I keep wondering what he would say to the guy he rented this boat from. How would he explain it?"

"Maybe he wouldn't have to," I said. "And maybe I've been going about this the wrong way. I've been looking for one boat in a thousand. Maybe we should be looking for one man in a thousand."

"You mean who the hell would rent to Tuco."

"No. Who would he ask? Tuco doesn't know the Delta any better than you or I do."

"So who does he know that knows the Delta?"

"You know who he knows. Who takes you guys fishing?"

"De Gama!" Floyd said.

"Correct."

De Gama was a World War II vet that Floyd had found in his travels. He took out boatloads of disabled veterans fishing on the Delta every year. Floyd and Tuco were regulars. I'd never met the man, but I've heard a lot of stories from Floyd and Tuco. They said he loved grunts because he understood what they had to do. On June 6, 1944, he was a young bosun's mate who motored three boatloads of G.I's to Omaha beach. He got the grunts off but lost his boat on the third trip.

"He hasn't got a telephone," Floyd said. "He lives aboard his boat at a marina near Rio Vista."

"Want to come along?"

"Can't. I'm cooking dinner for a lady friend, and besides it's a long shot, Duvall."

"It's a shot," I said.

It was a bull's-eye.

Two hours later I introduced myself to Joe De Gama, a tall and slender, white haired man with a slight stoop. I guessed he was in his mid eighties. Ten minutes later he was showing me the boat.

"I found the hull rotting near a bridge pier at Crockett," said De Gama. "I claimed it as salvage. Took me five years to restore it. I couldn't get anything like the original engine so I put in one of those light weight Japanese diesels. Runs a treat."

"Did Tuco know about this?"

"Sure. He helped. Took us a couple of days to put in that engine. And he helped me test it. He borrowed a junker so we could put it aboard and see how much water it drew. This is a little larger than the one I lost on trip number three. This was designed to carry a motorized vehicle."

Floyd was right. Folks would see this vessel, know what it was, but never think about it hauling freight. Perfect for his purpose, Tuco had known the boat, a fully restored, Higgins hull painted steel gray with the famous drop ramp in front, a World War II landing craft.

"When I started, I thought maybe I'd make it into a nice houseboat," De Gama said. "I decided to restore it first. Maybe went a little overboard. It will never be a houseboat now. I'm too old to finish it."

"This is a beautiful restoration," I said. "Maybe the San Francisco Maritime Museum would take it."

"Maybe," the old man said. "I'm not quite ready to let it go."

"So tell me what Tuco said to talk you into becoming a thief."

"Well nothing like that," De Gama said. "The word thief was never mentioned. He said it would be one last adventure, one last chance to save the life of a grunt, his friend Newton. It wasn't really stealing, he said, it was more like pulling the fangs out of a rattlesnake."

"So you went just like that." I said.

"Why not," said De Gama. "My family wants me to move into town, but they can't make me do it, as long as I'm good for useful work. When I'm scraping a boat or calking a hull, I kind of forget my arthritis. I kinda forgot that night too."

"How did you find the channel?"

"Well Tuco marked the channel. We had walkie talkies. I came down the main channel with running lights. He confirmed it was me. I turned off the running lights.

"He had these funny stick things that glow in the dark. He tossed a couple on both sides of the channel and lit up his skiff too. All I had to do was follow him in."

Tuco took a real chance lighting up that skiff, but maybe he'd been tooling around the island in the dark with glow sticks for the week before. Glowery's men might be used to it. Still he was taking a chance. If something went wrong he was the obvious target. He was just like the El Tee on the night of the pigs, holding up that damned strobe light at the height of his reach when he still thought they weren't pigs. I got goose bumps.

"Then what happened."

"It was all pretty normal. He showed me where to come in. I jammed her into the mud and dropped the ramp. He and Newton went up, started the van, and drove it aboard. I lifted the ramp on the winch and backed out of the mud. The diesel was really roaring.

"There was someone with a flashlight up on one of the houses. Maybe he couldn't see anything, or maybe he didn't quite believe what he did see."

"And you motored back here to Rio Vista?"

"Yeah. It took an hour or two."

"Joe," I said. "This is important. Did you see what was in the van?"

"Never did. I never looked," he said. "You know how Tuco is. When he tells you something's important you don't ask why.

"When we got back here we offloaded the truck at the boat ramp. I took them to my home boat and made them breakfast. It was Sunday, and I like to go to church with my nephew in Oakland. I got in my pickup; they got in the van. We were playing tag with each other all the way down Highway 4. We turned on the Interstate together, but he turned off at the Richmond Parkway."

"Anything else you think you can tell me?" I asked after a minute.

"Can't think of anything." he said.

"This was a real pleasure," I said. I shook his hand. "Thank you for trusting me. Thank you for showing me the boat. Think seriously about the museum." I nodded at the newly painted hull. "This is a fine piece of work."

"Thank you for saying so, son. Why don't you come out with Floyd and Tuco next time I do the fishing trip?"

I wondered how many fishing trips he had left in him. I wondered if Floyd and Tuco would ever come fishing together again.

CHAPTER 16

After dinner I called Lily in Fremont. I brought her up to date on the case and asked her to pass it on to Karen and the family.

"Frankly," I said," I'm running out of ideas. I can't bring myself to write to the woman I found in Tuco's email. If you guys think of anything, let me know. The best thought I've got isn't much. Much of the original paperwork on the Newton case is out in storage. I thought I'd go out there tomorrow and have a look. Maybe I'll see something that will lead to another thought."

Don't worry about it," Lily said. "You just need a little luck. With you I've noticed some usually turns up."

I took my time the next morning because I didn't feel very lucky. I was now grasping at slight straws, but for the moment they were the only straws I had. There was no reason to hurry my morning. If there was nothing there; there was no place else to look, and I preferred postponing my disappointment.

I didn't go out for breakfast. I ate my oatmeal and drank my morning coffee at the table in Floyd's garden reading the Contra Costa Times.

A big orange cat came through Floyd's fence, sat, curled his tail around his body, and watched me eat. When the oatmeal was gone, I put my bowl on the ground. The cat approached cautiously, not yet quite certain of me, but tempted by milk. When the milk was gone, I stroked the orange head and ears and was rewarded with a loud purr.

The cat wrapped himself around my ankles, but he seemed to have no interest in my lap. After a while he wandered out among the plantings still purring some of the time. I took a second cup of coffee and indulged myself in the sunny peace of the morning until the cat pounced and trotted proudly from among the flowers with a fat gopher.

A good omen, I decided. Peace officers are predators too.

I washed my dishes and left them to dry in the rack. I retrieved the card key for the storage place from a file box and headed out. I've rented the storage unit for many years. The yard is pretty big, at least a couple of acres circled by a high barbed wire fence, lined row upon row with metal sheds, most retired railroad cars.

The main office, a large industrial metal building with smaller lockers, guards the entrance. To enter the yard you slap your card key against a sensor and a motorized gate rolls open so you can drive among the aisles to your unit. Getting out is simpler. There's a button on a post inside that opens the gate.

I rent one half of an old railroad car on aisle D number 197. I've got an aluminum boat in there and a boat motor on a stand. Lily keeps her grandmother's china here, old silver, and albums of photographs of tough Irish men and beautiful women. All are boxed and stacked against the wall on the right.

On the left I opened the top drawer of a four drawer file cabinet. I grabbed the Newton folder, and tossed it in the front seat of the car. I boxed the cases more than five years old from the bottom drawer and put them on the floor of the car. I had some sorting to do. For tax purposes I could shred them all, but some cases were more sensitive. I needed to keep anything that might one day bite me worse than the IRS.

I closed the door of the storage shed, closed the hasp, and squeezed the padlock until it clicked. I found myself staring at the name on the lock, Schlage.

I have tinnitus, many old soldiers do. The ringing in my ears was suddenly very loud and I could hear my heartbeat.

I got back into the car very slowly. I was on aisle D. Aisle C was the next one closer to the gate. In aisle C I noted the numbering system and turned right. Not quite certain I remembered the number correctly, I pulled out my wallet, unfolded the envelope and verified the number, 237.

The lock was a Schlage like mine; indeed maybe it was, since Tuco had the free run of tools and hardware at my house.

I held my breath as I inserted the key from the envelope and turned it smoothly in the lock and opened the door. I breathed again. There it was.

The van stood alone in the old freight car. The space was more than long enough and almost too narrow, but Tuco had flattened a wing mirror and parked the van tightly against the right hand wall. The driver side door was unlocked, but the interior lights only flickered dimly. The battery was sure to be all but dead. The windows were all dark with dust and there was too little light from the open door of the shed to see much.

I got a flashlight from the glove box of my car before I squeezed through the driver side door, found keys in the ignition and the shift in park. Turning the key I got faint clicks from the starter, but the engine wouldn't turn.

I twisted in the seat to play the flashlight over the cargo. What a mess. Nothing was crated, probably to save space and weight, and there were spares for key parts still covered in comsmoline and dust. There were at least two mortar plates and three tubes. There were two intact 50 caliber machine guns and several spare barrels. There were at least half a dozen M-60 machine guns, a motley collection of M-16's and AK-47's with mortar rounds and belts of machine gun ammo everywhere.

The Mexican drug cartels were at war not only with each other, but also with the civil government. The contents of this van offered far more firepower than they had at present. Maybe Glowery was selling them more than firepower; maybe he was selling his expertise. Everything in there was Vietnam era weaponry that he knew how to service and use, all the tools he needed to make a small hell on earth.

That wasn't my idea of retirement. Running a muscle and drug racket was probably a softer job, but after all it was Ghost making the choice, Ghost who was so eager to take a chance for a bigger kill long, long ago. Tuco and I will carry the scars of Vietnam always, but I think Ghost joined us with scars already in place.

I pulled some tools from my car, popped open the engine compartment and removed the battery. The battery looked old. Maybe it wouldn't hold a charge. If not I'd buy a new one. Ghost would need to drive the van, if I let him have it.

I had tricky planning to do. Maybe I'd let him have the van; maybe not. Once Ghost had the van what would he need me for? I'd need to keep him at a safe distance and away from his hired help. It turned out in the end that I worried for nothing. In the end the hardest part was persuading the yard manager to program a card key for me that would let me into the yard after eight o'clock at night.

Group was scheduled for the afternoon, and I was glad of it. "This isn't exactly about combat," I said when it was my turn. "I've got a choice. Maybe a choice like a combat choice. I'm damned if I do and damned if I don't."

"I don't believe in the no win situation." MACSOG said.

"Serve the needs of the group and not yourself." HP chuckled.

"Okay so we've all watched Star Trek," I said. "That doesn't help. Tuco's involved. He's made a good-of-the-many choice, but it wasn't good for him. I think that's why he's hiding out. I think he's hiding from the law too. He stole something. He stole it from outlaws, but even having the stuff is illegal."

"What stuff?"

"For example, there's at least two fifty's."

"Fifty's?" HP asked.

"Machine guns. You remember those?"

"Holy shit."

"If I give the load back to the outlaw, maybe Tuco can come home."

"I vote for that. Let's get Tuco home." MACSOG said.

"But think about the outlaw. What do you think he'd

want to do with a fifty?"

"Shoot something - or somebody."

"I'm with Captain Kirk," Al said. I don't believe in the no win situation. If you think you've got a lose or lose choice, you're framing the problem wrong. Find a way to cheat. There's a third way."

CHAPTER 17

I mulled over things for three days before I was ready. In the middle I had an unplanned interruption.

My phone rang while I was on the freeway. I checked it when I pulled into the garage. There was no message, but I recognized the telephone number. For several years it was my office phone. I pushed the send key and put the phone to my ear.

"Chief Dornacker's Office."

"Is that you, Clair? He's got you answering the telephone? This is Duvall."

"Hi, George. Hang on. I know he wants to talk to you."

Dornacker said without introduction, "You need to come down here. There's been a new development."

"Glowery or Hodiak?"

"Tuco Ruis," Dornacker said.

"I'll be down," I said. "It will take me about an hour."

"What's keeping you?"

"Time and distance. I'm not punching a clock anymore. I've got to wash up and do my hair so I'll look good at your office."

"Get here as soon as you can," Dornacker said and hung up the phone.

Maybe Dornacker thinks all cops should be rude and he needs practice. I think he's already perfect.

I didn't dawdle. Once I 'd made myself presentable, the drive to the station took only twenty minutes, a good twenty minutes short of my hour estimate.

Sergeant Clair Rainford was on the desk today.

We shook hands. "It's been a while, Clair."

"I heard you dropped in."

"I'm glad to see that Dornacker hasn't turned you into a secretary in uniform."

"Nah. He wants the desk to screen his calls though."

"Would you tell him I'm here?"

"Sure. Have a seat in Interview Two. He'll join you there shortly." She looked left, right, and then back to me. "George he won't be alone."

"Thanks," I said, and made myself at home in Two.

Dornacker was uniform and accompanied by a younger man in shirt, tie, blue blazer and gray slacks came into the room.

"This is Major Mike Elrond," Dornacker said. "Major Elrond this is George Duvall." I'm not sure quite how, but Dornacker's voice gave my name some extra importance.

Elrond's hair was close cropped. I would guess he was in his early thirties. We shook hands and he handed me his badge and I.D., Criminal Investigation Command. He had handed me the badge with his left hand. I noted that the tip of his left little finger was missing; this was the El Tee's nemisis, the man who had pursued Recon all around the country.

I asked, "What can CID tell me about Tuco Ruis, also known as Jorge Jesus Luis Ruis?"

"Very little, I'm afraid," said Major Elrond, "but we'd like to ask him some questions. I'd like to ask you some too."

Dornacker had sandbagged me.

"About what?" I asked.

"We'd like to understand events in your Recon Platoon during the last week of January 1971."

"None of your business, Major. That was a combat mission. CID doesn't investigate combat."

"Except when there's strong reason to believe a crime may have occurred."

"You believe a crime occurred?"

"We don't know what to believe. There have been allegations."

"I recall no allegations, though we lost a civilian that week in a combat action. This was the middle of the jungle along a dirt road that was little more than a trail. We usually didn't see civilians. That's why I remember it. I was with the platoon for few more months after that and there were never any questions asked."

"There have been now."

"A little late, don't you think? I can't reliably remember what I had for breakfast two days ago. You want me to tell you what I remember from 35 years ago?"

"You do remember the incident. We are asking about the civilian who died. Your platoon leader reported her as a casualty of a predawn firefight."

"That's correct. I more or less remember what he said."

"Did you have any reason to believe his report was incorrect?"

"Certainly nothing factual."

"Factual?" Elrond asked.

"Well you know how it is," I said. "Things get pretty foggy in a fight. Sometimes you know the bit you were in, but mostly not much else. We were in the dark. There was shooting. We were surrounded by enemy movement. In the morning the civilian was dead."

"You didn't kill her?"

"Certainly not. You have my Lieutenant's report."

"He said she was in the charge of your squad. Could any of them have done it?"

"Not to my knowledge." Now maybe I knew how President Clinton felt dithering over the word 'is',"

"Do you suspect anyone?"

"I'm a cop too, Major. I suspect everyone until I get the evidence. There is no evidence, Major. Why would anyone make this out to be a murder? We were in a firefight. She got killed. Period. End of sentence. Why would anyone question this, especially years after the fact?"

"Some have said you weren't being shot at."

"You ever been in a night action, Major? Not only was it night, but we were in a damned jungle. You're too young to know about jungles in the night. You can't see a damn thing, and some of us probably weren't being shot at. There was a whole squad pointed at the trail. They weren't shot at. All the noise was behind them facing elements of two squads."

"I have it on good authority," the Major said, "There were no enemy shots fired, and in the morning there were no bodies, only pigs."

"You're right. They got away clean. They did that a lot. Some of us figured they drove pigs at us as a distraction so they could slip past us in the dark."

"But there were no incoming rounds."

"No one in Recon ever said that," I said.

They would never have said it and not because of some all for one and one for all bullshit. Loyalty doesn't really account for it, maybe only fear. Nobody wants to know anything worse than what they remember. Nobody wants to remember his doubt, anxiety, or pain. You want to remember the triumphs. You're sure to remember the dramatic defeats, but you try not to remember what you might fear to be true when no one could possibly be sure.

"There was gunfire, grenades, and claymores going off," I said. "How were you supposed to tell? We were only folks on the ground. Who could tell you anything different? There was nobody there but us!"

"And therefore no one was shooting at you," the Major said. "You were alone in the jungle confronted by a herd of pigs. One of you killed your prisoner."

But I got it. There was only one way he could be certain that no one was shooting at us, and suddenly I knew how.

"Even if we did, why would you be looking into it?"

The Major smirked. "It was murder after all."

"But apparently you didn't think so until sometime lately. It's been 35 years. If you didn't think it was murder, why would the Army embarrass itself by trying to investigate it now? CID doesn't usually investigate combat deaths. Why would you do it now?"

"There was a murder."

"Whatever made you think so? I can't imagine you were all poring over antique after action reports. I can't imagine that anyone in Recon would raise the accusation. Maybe some poor guy in a loony bin confessed to a murder, but he might confess to one whether one was done or not. You needed a smoking gun, Major, and I'm not at all sure that you think you have it."

"I'm here to question you, not to be questioned."

"Okay no questions. Why don't I just give you my best guess? I'm pretty sure you've got only dubious reasons to ask me questions."

Elrond leaned back in his chair, and folded his hands over his stomach. "Give it your best shot," he said.

"I certainly will," I told him. "In fact you'll get no more out of me unless you can prove me wrong."

Elrond shrugged.

"Dornacker," I said. "Did you get a letter, an email, or any other form of warning that the Major was coming here?"

Dornacker snorted. "I didn't need one. This department has always co-operated with other investigative agencies."

"Yes we have. Usually they have the courtesy to tell us they're coming in advance."

"He brought credentials."

"Yes he did, but they're deceptive."

"That's a real CID badge."

"Yes it is, but ask him for a telephone number where we can verify his job with his commander."

"I work in the CID headquarters at Quantico Virginia," Elrond said.

"That's a Marine base, not Army," Dornacker said.

"True enough," I said, "but none the less that's where the Army's CID headquarters are.

"If you're headquarters staff, you don't really work as an investigator anymore. Or did you ever, Major?"

"I said I work on the headquarters staff."

"And not in the field," I said. "But you've been out in the field for quite some time, a guy with the tip of his little finger left hand missing. You've been interviewing everybody in Recon no matter where they were all around the country.

"I'm surprised your boss has got such a big travel budget. Or is it because of budget that you have to do this?

"Dornacker, what do you do that isn't done by street cops? You do it and your Deputy Chief does sometimes, but you're scrupulous that investigators and street cops never do it.

"Trend analysis," said Dornacker, as if he hoped that was the right answer.

"I mean like in front of city council."

Dornacker grinned. "Politics," he said. "Politics."

"Correct," I said, "Just like headquarters staff. I imagine you're quite good at it, Major.

"If some Undersecretary of the Army gets caught in the bedroom with his gal Friday, Undersecretary gets censured or resigns, and training must be done, Army wide training. Even if she was willing, she was the Undersecretary's secretary so it's sexual harassment and the Army must demonstrate it is pro-actively opposed to sexual harassment, so everyone, General down to private E-1 must be trained to recognize it."

"Politics," Dornacker sighed.

Elrond began to seem uncomfortable. He had begun to fidget.

"A little while ago I made a mistake, didn't I, Elrond?"

"Perhaps you made several."

"Maybe, but this one was a doozie. I said that no one but Recon could have told you there were no incoming bullets, no one in Recon could be sure so they wouldn't tell you that, and I said there was nobody else there but us.

"Who else was there, Dornacker?" I asked.

"How would I know? I wasn't there."

"Well use a little logic. I said we were alone. That might not be strictly true. There was always someone we were looking for, and sometimes they found us and we didn't know they were there."

"The Vietnamese," Dornacker said.

"Yeah," I said. "The Vietnamese, the VC, or the NVA. Elrond here has launched a murder investigation because the enemy says they didn't shoot."

"He's a senior member of their diplomatic corps," Elrond said.

"I'm sure he's very senior, very official and very political. Why is a Vietnamese senior diplomatist talking to Army CID? Probably he isn't. He's talking to someone in the State Department, and some Statie is talking to a General pretty high up, and that makes it political, and oh, I forgot: We said Elrond wasn't an investigator. He's headquarters staff, a political fix it man."

Elrond shrugged. "You can't insult me. I'm just doing my job."

"Of course I can't insult you. Let me insult the job. You're not supposed to solve anything. You don't even know why this Vietnamese guy wants this. This is just like sexual harassment training. You're not changing anything, but you're making sure the Army, through the CID, can prove it was thorough."

"I intend to file a complete report," Elrond said.

"And you don't care what the conclusions are, do you? In fact I wouldn't be surprised if your commander had pulled you aside and suggested a white wash. Not a cover up, mind. Talk to everyone. Document their denials, and in the end you'll just say there's not evidence the gook is right."

Elrond was calm, perhaps even curious. "Why is it every Vietnam vet acts like a whack job paranoid?

"Let me tell you something you've overlooked. I'm not just a cop. I'm a very good cop. My commander thinks I'm his best detective. I don't have this job because it's political. I have this job because because it's important and I'm the best man for the job.

"Chief Dornacker tells me you were a good cop too. And you were a Chief. I'll bet you've made some decisions about who best to assign to sensitive work. That's what happened here. I've got the budget, the authority, and means to get this done. If murder was done I will find the killer. If not, I'll take a stab at proving you're all innocent."

"You can't prove a negative," I said.

"Perhaps not to absolute certainty, but I may not have to. Your friend who left town looks good for it. I'll know better when I have talked to the rest of your platoon including him. I will find out. I won't do a cover up. The result could have international importance. We can't sweep it under the rug."

"How many of us have you talked to so far?" I asked.

"You're number twenty two."

I decided I'd better keep him away from the El Tee and his list.

"I want you to tell me what you know," he said.

"I've told you. I don't know anything."

"You know your friend Ruis has taken off."

"Yeah I turned in a missing person report. I don't know where he is. But what's the big deal? Maybe I just pissed him off."

Elrond smiled. "I think not. Obviously you knew to expect me. You knew about this." He held up his hand with the missing fingertip. "You told me; I didn't tell you. You told me I was traveling around the country talking to your platoon."

I had blown it. I was angry and too intent on protecting Tuco.

"There is a rumor," I said carefully.

"So you're in touch with some of the other men?"

It's illegal to lie to a federal investigator. "Yeah."

"Some one told you I was coming?"

"Yeah. A guy missing the tip of his little finger."

"So you're talking to some of the men?"

"Yeah."

"Then you know something, I don't. You know phone numbers, names and addresses."

He handed me a yellow legal pad.

"Write them down."

"I can only remember names," I said. "And lots of those are only nicknames."

"So how do you find a phone number when you want to call?"

"I don't call. I don't want to call. I get called."

I almost told him that it was the El Tee that called, but may be that would put the El Tee at the top of his list. I knew what would keep him satisfied, and I I knew better than to lie to him or evade. He would get the list one day in any case if he kept talking to everyone he could find.

"There's a spreadsheet with contact information on my laptop," I told him. I can email it to you if you like."

He gave me his business card. "That will do nicely. Have you tried to email your friend Ruis?"

"I don't think I can. He left his computer behind as if he didn't expect he'd have much use for it."

"Interesting. He's hiding someplace without even a telephone. If you find him, give me a call, or get him to call me. He's not doing himself any good hiding out."

Later after I sent the spreadsheet to Elrond, I called the El Tee and told him about it. At first he wanted to cuss me out, but he calmed down once I explained.

"Nobody really knows anything," I said. "And all of them are loyal to the unit. Look how they've cooperated with you. They may believe things, but they don't *know* anything. They won't speculate because they won't do anything that might make trouble for anybody in Recon. Nothing will come of this, but Elrond will have answers – dead end answers, but all the answers he's going to get."

"You'd better be right, Duvall."

"Its not truth or consequences, El Tee. It's truth or nothing. I'm betting he'll go bust."

CHAPTER 18

The plan relied on Ghost more than I liked, but what are you going to do? I found the Glowery business number in the phone book, but someone else answered when I called. I told the voice I wanted to speak to Glowery.

"Maybe he ain't here."

"So take a message."

"I gotta pencil. Go ahead."

"Tell him Rogers Rangers."

"I'll tell him Mr. Rangers."

"I'm not Mr. Rangers. That's just the message I want you to give."

"We'll call you back."

In the old days I might have insisted Glowery had to come to the phone because I wouldn't leave a number. Unfortunately that bluff's no good since the phone company started selling caller I.D.

"Well do it soon," I said. "I don't think Mr. Glowery would like any delays."

I didn't have to wait long. My caller I.D. showed a number only slightly different than the one I'd called.

"Hello," I said.

"Who is this?" growled Glowery.

"It's your old Army buddy, Ghost," I said.

"Blondie! What's up."

"A Ford Econoline van."

"Does she carry cargo?"

"Well I didn't have an inventory" I said, "but I think it meets your requirements. There's a problem though. It's locked." It was now. I had locked it. "You'll need a key to drive it off."

"I've got a fucking key," Glowery shouted. "It's my fucking van! Every fucking thing in it is mine."

"Well why don't we meet alone somewhere and talk about it?"

"Where?"

"The coffee bar in the Barnes and Noble bookstore at Emeryville. Bring the keys," I said.

"That ain't alone."

"I will be," I said, "and I'm betting I'll be able to tell if you are.

"Why should I trust you?"

"Why indeed. But that's not the question. I can't trust you. You're not the trustworthy type. I'm a Dudley Do Right. You can trust me."

"Okay. When."

I put a finger on the end key of the phone so I could quickly cut him off.

"Half an hour," I said. "And bring some money. Five grand."

I pushed the key. I didn't want him to argue about the money.

He would barely have time enough to get from El Sobrante to Emeryville and certainly no time to set up anything tricky. He kept his arms shipment a close secret even from Hodiak who didn't want to know it. He was likely to come alone.

I bought a cup of coffee, sat down and pretended to read an interesting book about falconry. The coffee bar at Barnes and Noble can be a crowded place even at night. Three other people sat at my large table, all with coffee, two had laptop computers on, and two had books. The one with both a computer and a book kept glancing from page to screen and back again.

Maybe demanding money was a mistake. Maybe it wasn't. I didn't think Ghost could trust me if I didn't ask for money. He'd offered. He'd told me he wanted me to work for him.

I glanced at my watch. It was 7:39 p.m. Twenty nine elapsed minutes. I decided I would give him five more.

"This ain't alone," Ghost hissed as he slid into the chair next to me.

"Functionally it is," I said. "I don't know any of these people, and I'll bet you don't either. We can have a private talk, just you and me. Keep your voice low."

Glowery was nicely dressed, low cut walking shoes, black jeans, a white, long sleeved mock turtle tee shirt, and carefully tailored sports jacket that almost hid the piece under his left arm.

"So how's this going to work," he said.

"Real simple," I said. "We both must be cautious."

Ghost grinned. That didn't put me at ease. He looked twitchy. There was something wrong with his eyes. Maybe he'd been sampling some of his own products. He wasn't dressed like a biker gang leader, but if he was cranked up like one he was less predictable and more dangerous.

"Where's my van?" he asked.

"In a big metal shed, a storage locker in a storage yard surrounded with a barbed wire fence." I said.

"Shed got a number?"

"Uh-huh."

"You got a key?"

"Take this. It opens the shed," I said.

"It's just a padlock key. That won't get us in the yard."

"But it will get you into the shed," I said. "It's the only key that will. I don't have another. Now you're the only guy who can open that door."

"Okay. So how do we get in the yard?"

I'd carefully marked the card keys in my wallet to make sure I would give him the right one. "You know what this is?"

"Yeah. I seen guys use them at a parking garage."

"You know the drill. You slap this card against a reader somewhere. You probably saw it raise a gate arm at the parking garage. Where we're going it will open a rolling gate. You're going to use that to go through the gate when all the other customers are gone. I made a deal with the yard boss. That's what the five grand is for."

"How do we pay him?"

"I already did. Did you bring the money?"

He gave me the manic grin again. "I'll have to write you a check," he said. "I don't carry that kind of cash. I might run into some bad company."

"Okay," I said. "I know you're good for it." Of course he wasn't but I had to make him think I trusted him.

He winked at me. "Damned right, I am." Still more broadly he grinned.

Maybe it was his perfect teeth. I remembered others, the broken stubs and the cut away lips of Newton's body. I felt nauseous, and I could feel fear sweat on my forehead. I couldn't let Ghost see that. He was too much addicted to making others fear him. I swept my hand up over my forehead as if to sweep my hair back.

I glanced at my watch. It was after 8 o'clock.

"Let's go," I said. "You can leave your wheels here. Nobody will mess with them. The movie theater here won't let its last customers out until well after midnight, and you'll want to stash your van somewhere and come back for them."

"Slow down," Glowery said. "How do I know this isn't some cop trap? How do you know I won't just pop you and keep my five grand?"?

"I told you it was simple," I said. "Easy, peezee. "

"Write my check while we're driving, and put it in my glove compartment. There's a flashlight in there. Take it. You might need it, even though the yard is pretty well lit. At the yard you use your keys to go in. I'll drive away."?

"Like hell you will. Caught in that yard I'll look like a thief."

"Looks aren't everything," I said, "but no you won't. You've got legitimate keys that worked. Sure it's after hours, but did you know that? You've got no tools to break into anything. You're just there after hours trying to remember the number of your storage unit. At worst you're busted for trespassing and maybe carrying concealed, both misdemeanors."

"So when do I get the locker number?"

I handed him my business card.

"Just as soon as you convince yourself this isn't a trap. Check everything out and when you know it's safe, you call my cell number on that card. I'll tell you what it is while I drive away. I don't want to be within miles of you when you pick up that load."

"And if I won't let you go?"

"Then you'll never know the number on the container."

"I'd try them all."

"You might not find it. You only have a couple of hours before the dogs show up. There are hundreds of containers out there. If you shoot the dogs you'd have to explain yourself, and what would be the point? Do it my way. I'm making this easy for you."

"If you ain't setting me up to take a fall some other way."

"Why would I do that? Nothing in it for me. Hodiak says he'll kill me if I queer your deal."

Ghost grinned wolfishly. "Fucking right. He would. And if he didn't I'd take you both out."

"Take it easy, Ghost. You don't need to try to scare me. I'm scared. We're both getting something here. You're getting your load. I get you off my back. I get Tuco."

"No deals. You can rot for all I care, but if I cross paths with that son of a bitch again, he's going down."

"No deal needed. Tuco will never see you again. I looked at your load. I know you're going to Mexico, and you're never coming back. You're in a hurry. You've been in a hurry from the beginning, maybe all your life. There's killing to do in Mexico and nobody to stop you. It's all you dream of.

"I give you the load and I don't have to trust you. You'll leave Tuco alone because you're leaving town. I want to give you this load. It's in my own interest to do it."

"You're just giving me the load? What's the five grand for?

"To bribe the yard manager. I get nothing. I'm just giving."

"And you're not setting me up?"

"How can I do that? I'm the guy taking all the chances. Once I show you the yard you could kill me for dessert and find the locker later."

This got me another cold eyed grin. "I was never squeamish in the 'Nam, Blondie, and I'm not now; I've had more practice."

"Try to make me an exception," I said. "I'm of more use as a partner than an opponent."

"Want me to drive?" he asked. "Just to make sure I don't pull any stunts.

"Hell no," I said. "This car is my baby, and I know you won't pull any funny stuff. Have you already forgotten you're writing me a check?"

He wrote it promptly, waving it in front me as I drove so I could see where he had written in the numbers.

As we rolled up Interstate 80, fog was rolling in over the bay. The night was too chilly to have the top down. I drove at moderate speeds in the middle of the freeway. I didn't want to get either of us more excited than we already were so I kept a steady pace, Richmond Parkway to Giant, left turn, right turn over the tracks and there we were.

I parked, and we got out.

"Card reader's right over there," I pointed.

"What if it doesn't start," Glowery said.

He meant the van. I knew it would start because I bought the new battery, but he didn't know that and he was right to worry.

"I hadn't thought of that," I lied. "I couldn't try it without a key. It shouldn't matter. You can call anyone you like. You've got the keys."

He nodded and reached out. I shook his hand. "So long, Blondie," he said.

He turned away and then turned back. Now his automatic was in his hand, the barrel pointed low at my stomach which flooded with adrenaline seemed to shrink back against my spine.

"You're going with me."

"No I'm not. If I go with you, I'll be dead. I'm a guy you can trust, but you're a killer."

"Which locker is it?"

"You won't find out if you kill me," I said.

"I don't have to kill you. I just have to hurt you."

"If you hurt me one of us dies. If you kill me you'll never know. If I kill you what does it matter?"

The barrel of his gun still hovered over my guts. My stomach was trying to get to the other side of my spine, and I imagined my testicles had probably shrunk to something like the size of peas.

He wasn't just watching me. There was some kind calculation going on. He kept staring out into the darkness behind me as if it could give him some answer or produce some hope of help that could not come.

Almost as quickly, he holstered the gun.

"Don't I scare you?" he asked.

"All the time," I said. "You always do. I've got no reason at all to want to fuck this up. Think it through. Your load's in there, or I lied about it. If I lied, if you don't get your load, I've only pissed you off. I know better than to do that so your load's gotta be there."

"So how do I know it's not a trap? You're still a cop. You've been a cop most of your life. We been living cheek to cheek for so long, I know who you are. I know how you think. You only bent the rules once that I know of, and that was before you were a cop."

"What do you want from me, Ghost?" I asked. "You don't have to trust anyone, not even me. You've got a couple of hours before the dogs. Check the place out. Check it out completely and give me a call when you're sure there's no trap."

I walked back to the car and breathed a sigh of relief that he let me get in it.

I took a right hand turn and pulled down the road a couple of blocks, parked and got out. I had a bulky leather jacket in the trunk that I traded for my sports jacket. I put on a ball cap to complete a change of profile.

Pretty sure of what I'd find, I took a look at Ghost's check. It was indeed made out for five grand, but paid to the order of "Fuck You Blondie," and signed "Ghost"

I pulled out my automatic and jacked a shell into the chamber. I carried the gun in my right hand against my thigh. Even if Ghost could see me from the yard or the parking lot he'd never see the gun. That certainly didn't arm me well enough once Ghost got to his van, but I'd tried to lull him in, and there was a chance he was trying to lull me. I couldn't be sure he was following my program.

I took my time approaching the parking lot. Once there I circled the perimeter checking the shadows and hiding places until I was sure they were empty. Ghost was apparently inside combing the aisles of storage containers for any sign of a set up or an ambush.

I settled behind a dumpster on the far side of the parking lot where I could look through the gate and down the central aisle that he'd have to use to drive out.

The longer aisles are L shaped, each wrapping around the corner of the property where the office and parking lot were located. The shortest aisles were closer, the aisle, D, where my container was located, was the longest since it wrapped around the length of two sides of the property. All of the aisles were the same length to the left of the exit aisle and longer to the right.

I caught a glimpse of Ghost as he loped from the long arm of B down the center aisle and then turned left down the short arm of aisle C. "He's in short C" I said quietly. After a few minutes when he'd crossed back over I said, "He's in long C." He was gone perhaps fifteen minutes before I announced he'd moved into short D. Long D took twenty minutes before he was through. I crouched down behind my shed when my telephone vibrated.

"What's the number?

"Are you satisfied you're safe?"

"Completely. Thanks again, Blondie."

"You're welcome. Stay out of my life. The number is C237"

After I ended the call, I said, "I'm shutting off now." I keyed the sequence on my telephone that killed the mike.

Sounds often carry much further at night. I could hear a loud squeal when he opened the metal door. He was careless now. He revved the engine a couple of times to make sure of it after he started the van.

I knew he would have to maneuver a bit in the container because of the way Tuco had jammed it against the right hand wall. A couple of minutes passed before I could see the splash of light from his headlights playing across the entrance/exit aisle.

Ghost turned into the central aisle where I could see him just as the small, command-detonated charges exploded to blow out his tires and kill his engine. Dark armored figures wearing shirts marked ATF poured from apparently locked containers.

"Richard Glowery you are under arrest. Come out of that van with your hands high and visible."

Maybe he thought he was doing Recon proud. He came out with an AK-47 popping on auto. I crouched behind my dumpster while Ghost died.

In the movies or on TV it's always the rookie cops who throw up. That night I proved veterans puke too. I hate killing, but I still do it. Ghost was slaughtered like a pig. There were as many as forty guys out there. They got him with way too many bullets. He was pretty torn up.

The shirts said ATF because they had the jurisdiction and the warrant. The FBI was there with their organized crime task force. They were joined by Richmond tactical, Alameda County SWAT, and selected officers who'd targeted Glowery for a very long time, Bob Schooner for one.

Schooner found me wiping my mouth by the dumpster. He pulled a bottle of water out of a leg side pocket and offered it to me. I rinsed out my mouth first and took a long drink.

"Thanks Bob. What about Hodiak?"

"Like you figured. He tried to tail you from Barnes and Noble. CHP pulled him over on a phony bad taillight. How did you know?"

"A guess," I said, trying not to feel too fatuous. "Let's just say I knew he had a vested interest. Glowery could trust him and maybe no one else. And Glowery was way too smart to just go along with what I said."

"I want to thank you, George. Do you know how much this means to me? I've been gunning for him for years."

"I know."

"They'll take me off the street now. I might even get a desk. I could play golf."

I was beginning to tear up now and grateful Schooner could not see it in the dark. Maybe I was a bit in shock. Maybe not. Maybe I shouldn't be so shocked. I could still mourn Ghost. He was an asshole all the way back to Vietnam, but he was Recon's asshole, which made him something like the brother you always have to beat up.

I was still holding the gun. I released the slide, jacked the live round out, reloaded the magazine, put it back in the gun, put the gun back under my arm, and began my two block walk to the car.

In the yard cops were stringing crime scene tape. I could hear a generator, probably for the big standing lamps lighting the disabled van and Ghost's mangled body. The doors of the van were all open. Weaponry spilled from the cargo in a tangled pile. The flash of cameras seemed constant.

I was very glad not to have any part of the investigative circus. Across three counties search warrants were being executed. Dornacker no doubt had a team at Glowery's El Sobrante house, and for first time San Joaquin County Sheriff deputies were invading Glowery's island. Chuck Wang had a front row seat.

There'd been so much gunfire, I knew there'd be stories on the late night news so I called Lily on her cell.

"The cops with my help took down Glowery tonight. He came back at them with an AK-47, and they killed him. It's bound to be on the broadcasts tonight. They might not have my name, but they will tomorrow. There's going to be a news conference, and I'll be there."

"I'm so sorry," Lily said finally. "I know you wouldn't have done that unless you had to, but you're probably feeling awful."

"Thanks Sweetie," I said. "I'll be okay. They weren't my choices, but Glowery made his own, and this last one was probably the best. He'd never make it in jail."

I drove back to Floyd's house and my cottage. I took a hot shower. Toweled dry and dressed for bed, I got some ice and poured myself a little V.O. When I poured my second, I called the El Tee. The phone rang many times. I expected to be shifted to voice mail when he growled, "Bookman."

"Ghost's dead," I said. "I set him up. Cops took him down."

"He was such a pain the ass," the El Tee said after a while. "He was so damned aggressive Sharkey was afraid to let him walk point. I remember Sharkey chewing him out. Sharkey told Ghost we were supposed to be sneaking up on people and not just looking for a fight. I'll never forget him sneaking up on that dude with a knife."

"Well he got a gunfight tonight," I said. "They hit him at least twenty times. They'd told him to come out with his hands up and empty, and he came out with an AK."

"Don't sweat it, Blondie. That's how Ghost would want to go. He was always a good man to send into trouble. Maybe he still is. Could we throw him to the C.I.D.?"

"Shooting always made him happy," I said. "I believe you're right. I believe I'm going to suck on another glass of whiskey and go to sleep."

CHAPTER 19

My alarm went off 3:30 a.m. The news conference was scheduled at six to catch the local morning news. Since the ATF was the lead agency, the resident agent in charge asked us all to join him in an auditorium at the San Francisco Federal building. I brewed my coffee, shaved, and dressed in a suit and tie. I left enough time to get there on BART.

I caught my train at Del Norte station at 4:46 and got off at the Civic Center station a little after 5:30. All through the short walk to the Federal Building, I wondered how I'd get in. Usually the doors weren't open before 6. I shouldn't have worried. There was a bleary eyed man still wearing his ATF tee shirt waiting for me at the door.

Cameras and crew were already in place. There was a small stage, a podium and a small forest of microphones. I guess the ATF did a press release the day before telling them about the early conference for "something very hot." My escort showed me to my seat in a ring of chairs behind the podium.

The agent in charge introduced himself and began to read a prepared statement. Hard copy was being handed among the press as he read.

Press conferences seem alike, a description of the events, introduction of the players, representatives of collaborating agencies and departments, television lights, camera flash, questions and answers.

Just routine, folks. Everyone did his job and we uncovered a major criminal conspiracy.

There was a slide show of photographed weapons. They'd assembled two of the fifties on tripods and stood up a couple of mortars for the T.V. cameras.

"Warrants are being executed as we speak, and we'll provide you with a complete inventory of the armament as soon as we can," the resident agent said.

I couldn't quite sleep through this. I'd asked to be there. Eventually, after the introductions and the long slide illustrated narrative of the night's events, the resident ATF agent said, "Chief Duvall would you please come forward and explain to these gentlemen how you came to discover Glowery's hoard of arms.

"Good morning, Ladies and Gentlemen," I said, "I think I can make this interesting for you."

I tried, but it had to be a tap dance. Maybe every press conference is the truth, but not the whole truth, the truth about things you know, and not so much about what you don't.

I wanted their attention because I wanted them to write stories, but I couldn't tell it all. "This all began for me because my friend Jorge Jesus Luis Ruis, also known as Tuco Ruis went missing."

I decided to give them something juicy they couldn't ignore.

"Tuco and I were in the service together. He was my radio telephone operator. I've never said this publicly before, but Glowery was in that platoon too."

I told them about Tuco's friend Newton, and I told them about Glowery's island and how they'd ripped Glowery off. I made excuses. "Tuco's like a lot of combat vets. He doesn't like cops or bosses much. Maybe he didn't do the right thing after he stole these guns. Maybe he should have simply called a cop or told the ATF about it. I think if Tuco and his friend Newton had done that, they might both be dead. Newton's dead anyway. Tuco had to run because he was scared that might happen to him. There was no limit to what Glowery might do. I was his solution to the problem of the guns. He left me the storage unit number and the key. I'm not always the brightest pup in the litter, so it took me a while to figure it all out."

I had a disclaimer.

"Some of you may know that Richard Glowery was a resident of El Sobrante during my entire tenure as Chief of the local police department. He was already well established as a person of interest in several drug and racketeering enterprises. I need not tell you that we watched him very carefully, and in El Sobrante, he was very careful too. In fact he may have done us some favors. I cannot recall the last time there was a complaint of violence or burglary in his neighborhood, and biker gentlemen in El Sobrante are unfailingly polite. We could never find a reason to arrest any of them."

Finally I wrote myself into the story as the hero.

"I've wanted this guy for years. He didn't blight my little town, but he was extraordinarily destructive in others, and he dishonored combat veterans like me everywhere. Once I found the van with its cache of weapons, taking him down was really a piece of cake.

"I wore a wire and arranged for the police to tap my cell phone. I told Glowery the van was locked, and he told us, on the phone tap, that he had a key and owned the van and all its contents. I offered him to trade my knowledge of where the van was for Tuco's life and we set a trap for Glowery when he took possession."

I got a barrage of questions afterward, but none of them made much of a mark on my basic story. None of them figured out how much I'd simplified the truth.

I'd managed not to tell them that Tuco had worked pretty hard at hiding his plans and activities from me so none of them asked the questions I couldn't answer. Why was he hiding from me? Why would Tuco risk himself on Glowery's island to get Newton out? If he was so scared of Ghost why'd he stick around for weeks after ripping him off?

I got what I wanted, or most of it. Glowery's take down made the national news, but none of the network broadcasts mentioned me or Tuco. Locally, I got better play, all of the stations mentioned that Tuco was missing, and the reporter on channel 7 actually closed his story by saying, "Now Tuco Ruis can safely come home."

Maybe.

1I had other business at the moment because I took Hodiak's threat seriously. There was a chance he'd be caught dirty when they executed the search warrants, but by noon the next day I knew they hadn't caught him, Hodiak was long gone. He'd said he'd have to run. Now I'd always have to carry my piece.

I took the rest of the day off. I called Lily up and made a dinner date. I picked her up in Fremont and drove back to Horatio's in San Leandro at the Marina. I hadn't enjoyed Horatio's pea salad for a long time, and I like their prime rib.

We took a room at the Fremont Hilton. I made her promise she'd let me take her home before midnight. I guess I'm puritanical enough that I don't think it should be too easy for my daughter or my grandchild to know when we were making love.

Afterward I collapsed in her arms and held her tight.

"Maybe now you've had enough," she said.

"Yeah. Now. Violent death is a funny kind of aphrodisiac," I said.

"I know," she said. "It's as if you reach for the best kind of proof you're still alive."

"How am I doing?"

"Oh, you're alive alright. How are you doing about Tuco? How long will it be before he comes home?

That isn't strange pillow talk for us. Sometimes I think Lily can read my mind, but the truth is when you've been together long enough how ever close you are, you also keep some boundaries. Maybe Lily didn't know it, but she was stepping on one now, but did I really want to keep it intact?

I didn't answer for a long time. I thought about a lot of things, my long friendship with Tuco, my nightmares, and my marriage. We wouldn't have much if we could only meet in hotel rooms for the rest of our lives.

Finally I said, "I'll wait a little while. But I don't think he'll be back tomorrow or the next day. I know this looks to be all about Glowery, but it's not. Glowery is just a side show; Tuco's the main event.

"He put himself in the dragon's mouth when he went to work for Glowery. He'd burned Glowery before, and it wouldn't take much for Glowery to burn him back. So why did Tuco do it?

"Maybe I know. Tuco told Newton something he'd never told anyone, not even me. He should never have told Newton. He should never tell anybody. He didn't even tell me. If Tuco did tell Newton he'd have to get him away from Glowery if there was a chance that Glowery could ever find out."

"What is it?" Lily asked. "What's his secret?"

"He never told me," I said. "I hope he never does."

"Why not?"

"Because I don't want what he'd tell me to be true, and as long as he doesn't tell me I can pretend it isn't."

"But you don't know. You only know what you think it is, whether he told you or not. How can you know if he never told you?"

I took a deep breath and let it out.

"It don't mean nothing," I said. "Which means it means everything. I know his secret; There were only two people who could have done it, and I know I didn't."

So I told her, finally, after 35 years.

CHAPTER 20

January 21, 1971

"This is an ambush. Listen when your Lieutenant speaks."

The El Tee waited. Squad leaders stopped talking. We had to concentrate to hear. No one in Recon spoke above a whisper until the shooting started.

"Listen up," the El Tee said. "NVA may be on this road, and we're supposed to blow them away if they show up."

North Vietnamese Army? Not fucking likely. We ran into NVA all the time in Cambodia, but we'd seen fewer bad guys than I had fingers since last June. This was January, 1971. Kissinger was in Paris talking peace. Why would the NVA want to mess with us?

"Third Squad, you guys are the base." the El Tee said. "Put your machine gun in the middle of your squad. Spread out about sixty meters. Make sure every man has a separate firing position and make sure he knows exactly where the guy to his left and right are. We can't be shooting at each other if we blow this thing.

"Second Squad, you take the left flank. Your sixty will anchor the left end of the ambush. Your gunner needs to know the right hand limit of his fire. Don't make a perfect triangle. I want you and Tuco in the closest hootch. Set up a little outside of Skeeter on the gun so you can cover his left flank.

"First Squad, you've got the same deal on the right. Your big gun anchors the ambush line on the right. Set up your hootch and position to defend the gun on the right.

"Second and First Squad, join your lines at the back and complete our perimeter.

"Blondie, you've got the Alpha Alpha. Aim it down our back trail, well left of your gunner. If they blow it, we'll have early warning, and maybe if they blow it we'll take some out with little or no risk to us. Like always, Blondie, show every guy the trip wire and make sure they all know exactly where the Alpha Alpha is."

As if I wouldn't.

Lately I always got the fucking Alpha Alpha. I knew how to use it better than anyone else, but I hated it, and the El Tee knew it. I wouldn't let anybody else in my squad set it up. The damn thing was too dangerous.

I got the Alpha from Rock, the Platoon Sergeant. The guys in the CP carried the parts of the Alpha Alpha. Even the El Tee carried one of the claymores. The only guy in the command post who didn't carry one was El Tee's RTO because he had the Prick 25 radio and the spare battery.

Soon, at my direction, Second Squad was hacking space out of the jungle. We were on the edge of a thick stand of bamboo, but here there was plenty of space between bamboo clumps. Since this wasn't triple canopy sunlight reached the ground. Wait-a-minute vines and weeds choked available space. Each guy wanted a dry space to sleep, something high enough to let the water run off if it rained and clear enough of rock and thorn that his air mattress wouldn't go flat.

I told Skeeter where to put his gun and helped him find a place for the hootch he shared with Alphabet. I left the Alpha Alpha with Tuco and told him to start fixing our spot. I went down to our end and made sure the last guys in Second were properly joined up with First Squad on our left.

None of these jobs was hard. I had the best squad in Recon, and I was fit to judge. I'd been in the bush for eight months. My guys knew their business. We worked well as a team. Except for a couple of newbie's we'd been keeping each other alive a long time. Teamed with "old" short timers, the newbie's would learn soon enough.

When all were in position we'd made good ambush line and a secure night defensive position, a triangle with slight bulges left and right along the road. The Command Post was secure, surrounded by the squads.

Walking down the line, I told each of the guys generally where I was going to put the Alpha Alpha.

"Tuco will be back to show you later," I said.

Tuco had spread out his poncho liner on the ground and was extracting mine from my pack.

"Let's get that later," I said. "We've got the Alpha."

Tuco groaned and swung the radio onto his back. The ANPRC-25 radio was a load, and we weren't quite yet at the end of a long day.

"I swear to God," he said. "When I get home I'm going to get me a Prick 25 of my own so I can set it on my back porch and piss on it anytime I like."

We loaded ourselves with gear and claymores, three each. We left our packs and night gear behind.

Tuco called the CP on the radio and told the RTO we were moving out to the left along the road for the Alpha Alpha. The El Tee's RTO repeated the report to the squads, in case they hadn't heard it when Tuco called it in.

I walked back to the guy on our left, Posthole, and told him where we were going, and asked him to pass it down the line. We went back right for Skeeter.

I told Skeeter he'd laid out a good set up for his Sixty.

Alphabet grinned.

Skeeter said, "Fuckin' A, Blondie, we didn't do it for you."

"I know. I'm still going to tell you when I think it's good." I told him where we were going, and pointed down the road to indicate where I thought the Alpha Alpha should be.

"If you see somebody over there it might be us."

By now we'd killed enough time the squad leaders would have passed the word to everyone else about where we'd be.

I heard a loud whisper, "Hssssst. Hey Blondie!"

I wasn't surprised to see the Ghost.

"I'm going out with you," he said.

Ghost wasn't in my squad. He didn't take orders from me, or from anyone else for that matter. Ghost did whatever Ghost wanted to, probably always had and always would.

His name's the thing. In Cambodia the whole platoon watched while Ghost silently stalked an NVA sentry, and killed him with a knife. He danced in swiftly and silent, clamped his hand over the mouth, jerked back the head, and sliced across the throat.

Someone had whispered, "Ghost who walks." He was a Ghost. What he did was useful. What bothered me was he liked it, but so what?

I said, "Thanks Ghost. We can use the help."

Tuco and I picked our way through about ten meters of jungle before we stepped out on Highway 3. I chose a spot for the Alpha. Tuco walked on another 15 meters and picked a spot with some cover and good concealment to cover me. Ghost walked on, disappearing silently into the jungle before the turn in the road. Usually you want every man accounted for. We wouldn't know where Ghost was but didn't care; he didn't need us to know.

The El Tee had put us on a long straight stretch of Highway 3, a red dirt road about five meters wide. We'd see them for more than a hundred meters if we had to blow the ambush. We walked twenty meters further.

Putting me on the Alpha Alpha again, the El Tee was telling me he was boss. I knew who boss was. Knowing was part of my job. Trouble was I didn't like the way boss was doing his job and I told him so.

Kissinger was in fucking Paris talking peace. Didn't that make it our job to do everything carefully with very little risk? As far as I was concerned the El Tee was a show boat. He always seemed too ready to volunteer us, and when he volunteered we were in for trouble. The El Tee was out to make a name for himself with the Colonel. So I'd told him and got put in charge of the Alpha Alpha.

Alpha Alpha was a soft name for a booby trap, the words radio shorthand for automatic ambush. We liked to call it an ambush because it wasn't. In ambush men decide when, how, and who to shoot. A booby trap makes no decisions; it simply kills.

The Alpha Alpha wasn't an innocent weapon. Grunts invented it; Division standardized it; and then discouraged it. No longer effective they said. Killed more grunts than gooks.

Maybe it was banned, but Recon still used it. We were different because we were alone. Recon was the only part of Echo that humped the bush. Echo Mortars were always stationed at the Fire Base. Echo Radar was at the Fire Base to detect intruders. Echo Recon was in the jungle looking for trouble. There were very few of us.

Our company commander was many miles away at company headquarters in the rear at Phouc Vinh. In the bush the Recon platoon leader took orders over the radio directly from the Colonel. We weren't humping with a hundred man line company. We didn't hump like line companies. We walked quietly and very fast. Mostly we didn't like line companies. They were noisy and slow. We couldn't trust them.

Since we were alone in the jungle most of the time, the El Tee and every Recon commander before him thought we needed the Alpha Alpha to guard our backs.

The Alpha Alpha was invented by grunts to avoid the dangers of a night ambush.

On night ambush a squad would usually set up next to a likely VC trail with several claymore mines. You could aim the mines. They were shaped charges with hundreds of pieces of shrapnel that stood on little legs. The kill side of the claymore was conveniently labeled, "Front Toward Enemy."

Tuco liked to say you shouldn't walk up on any claymore you could read. The mines were issued with a little hand held generator called a "clacker". There was a wire running from the clacker to an electrical detonator in the mine.

All you had to do was squeeze the clacker and any enemy close to the kill side would be dead.

The Alpha Alpha was set up the same way, but without the people. The clacker was replaced with a battery. The detonator circuit was interrupted by spring metal held apart by a bit of plastic spoon from the C rations. The spoon was connected to a trip wire which ran across the trail in front of the mines.

Set up wasn't difficult, but nerve wracking. If you made a mistake before you hooked up the battery the mines might blow and maybe kill you.

I was very careful and I took my time. I almost made a mistake. Our electrical wires were braided and one stray whisker almost completed the circuit. I cut it off with my jack knife before connecting the battery and then I took a breather. I checked both directions on the road. I could see Tuco, because I knew where he was. He nodded and gave me thumbs up.

I always test the trigger before I connect the detonator. I'd made a test light from a standard issue, olive drab, flashlight. I wired it in place of the blasting cap. I put the battery behind and out of range of the claymores, and I hooked the other end of the wires.

Back at the trigger, the test light was on. When I interrupted the circuit by pushing the handle of a plastic spoon between the contacts, the light went off. When I pulled it out, it went back on, several times. I disconnected the battery again.

I checked with Tuco again. Apparently everything was okay. No sign of movement. I'd been with Recon a long time now, and I wasn't used to walking around in plain view. Without cover or concealment, if Charley showed up, I'd be whacked for sure, if Tuco didn't whack 'em first.

I went back to Alpha Alpha and set up the trip wire. Rock, the Platoon Sergeant, got a spool of fishing line in the mail from his dad every couple of months. Usually some was still left in the old spool, and he gave it away to other units.

I tied one end of the fish line around some bamboo on the far side of the road. The line was tied across the road at least sixteen inches off the ground. I wanted to make sure the first guy to come to the wire couldn't accidentally step over it.

The other end had to be tied to the spoon so the trip wire was taut without pulling the spoon out to complete the circuit. That was easy enough to do. You tie the knot with a bit of slack and then move back the battery and trigger until the line was taut.

With the battery disconnected, I gave myself a break and lit a cigarette. I waved to Tuco to let him know there were now two of us alert. He gave me a thumbs-up and lit a cigarette too.

I always got nervous before the next step because this was the first chance something might blow up. I was sweating some now and not just from heat and exercise.

I felt lucky to have Tuco. I count on him. Part of me knew it wasn't luck, but it felt that way. If I couldn't trust him, I'd have found a way to get him out of Recon. We couldn't afford screw ups, but Tuco was better than not-a-screw-up. I could concentrate on my job and ignore everything else knowing he had my back.

I was sorry to finish the cigarette. I reminded myself the battery wasn't hooked up and the blasting cap wasn't in the circuit yet.

The El Tee always said this was all easy to do, if you knew what you're doing, and just did it. "Don't think too much," he said, "You damn hippie college grads just fuck yourselves up."

I didn't like him much either, but he was right. I thought about things too much. It didn't help. I have a vivid imagination, and I can't just whitewash the truth.

One stray electric spark and your blasting cap can blow when you hook it up. I didn't want to hold it and make an accidental circuit. I dropped off my ammo bag, and took my shirt off. I attached one wire from the battery to the cap, put the cap on down on the driest part of my shirt to insulate it from the ground. I hooked the other wire to the cap and retreated to the battery.

The cap didn't blow when I connected the battery. I disconnected it again. All that remained was to put the blasting cap in the fuse hole of claymore number one and put my shirt on.

A rock thumped the ground too damn close to my trip wire.

"Blondie," Tuco loudly whispered from his concealed position.

I grabbed my M-16 and flicked off the safety with my thumb, and scooped up my magazine bag.

An old woman rounded the bend of the road fifty meters further down the back trail. She saw me. I felt like I'd been dancing around Alpha Alpha forever. I stepped back into the woods. She'd know I was there, but if there was anyone with her, they might not know exactly where.

She was dressed in dingy rags and barefoot. Even at our distance, I was pretty sure she didn't have teeth, and I didn't want to smell her. There was a gory hole in the right side of her chest.

At least Tuco hadn't shot her. He could have. He still could. Ghost had let her go too. I began to wonder if he might have a conscience.

We were in a "free fire" zone. Commanders could shoot at their own discretion. The South Vietnamese government declared the area to be largely controlled by hostile forces. In effect they said there was nobody here, just the enemy and us.

One of the newbie's had asked what this meant. The El Tee said if it twitched we should shoot it twice, and then maybe we should examine the corpse to make sure it was dead. Ghost had grinned.

I didn't. As far as the South Vietnamese government was concerned there was nobody here. The Bronze Age folks who eked out a living farming jungle clearings were nobody. Nobody was there when the battalion did a combat assault on a jungle clearing to make our fire base. Nobody planted the crops in that clearing, and nobody was here to stop this, but us.

Tuco and I had talked this over. We had to. Soldiers killing civilians were a public scandal. Lt. Calley was on trial for the My Lai massacre at this very moment. We didn't care what the El Tee said or what twitched. We weren't killing any civilians, though maybe we'd die trying not to kill them.

I moved to Tuco's position and grabbed the mike.

"CP, CP," I said. "This is Dragon Two."

"Go ahead Two," said the CP RTO.

"Tuco and I are on the Alpha. We have movement. A lone Montagnard. She saw me. The Alpha's not armed yet. It won't blow."

"Why didn't you grease her, Two?" the El Tee asked.

"No reason, sir. She has no weapon. There's no one else. I'd like to bring the rest of the squad up to make sure of her."

"Negative Two. Remain in place or rejoin your squad. We'll let her walk into the ambush in case there's someone with her. Recon this is Dragon acknowledge."

We listened to the other two squads check in. I didn't bother. He knew I was listening.

"This is Dragon. Move into your firing positions. Dragon Two is out by the Alpha Alpha. He's got movement, a woman, unarmed. We'll wait until she has passed our position. I'm going to the Dragon One gun. When she passes I'll key the mike. You can fire if you have a target. If anyone shoots, everyone shoots. Otherwise listen for my command."

"Dragon One, Roger."

"Dragon Three, Roger."

I didn't say anything. Those were horseshit orders and the El Tee knew it. One itchy trigger finger in Third Squad, and the woman would be dead. Skeeter would get the word from Third Squad on the line. There was nothing I needed to tell any of the rest of the guys. They knew where I was. Except for Skeeter none of them was going to shoot because Tuco and I were somewhere in front of their guns. I might spook them if I moved back in, but there was good reason to move. If I could find an excuse I'd keep the woman from walking into the trap.

I'd need an excuse. The VC and the NVA sometimes drove the Montagnards as a screen. You saw only peaceful civilians, but you could step into the open and get whacked.

The woman moved down the road but slowly. As she came closer, Tuco and I could hear her. She moaned and grunted with every step and sometimes gave a sharp, loud cry as if her pain was suddenly worse.

She walked holding her hand over the hole in her side. Maybe she had a sucking chest wound. Maybe she held the hole closed to help her right lung work properly.

Nothing moved behind her, at least no one Tuco or I could see. Now she was more than thirty meters past the bend where the road disappeared. Surely our enemy wouldn't space themselves quite so far.

I couldn't decide what to do. I didn't want to step out onto the road unless I had to. The El Tee wouldn't shoot me, but he'd be pissed. He'd bring charges or slap me with an Article 15.

I got lucky.

The woman drew up beside our position. She stopped. She peered around at the jungle looking left and right. Finally she was staring right at us, though we had buried ourselves in brush. She sat down in the middle of the road.

"Dragon, this is Dragon Two."

"What you want Two?"

"She's not moving sir. She sat down in the middle of the road in front of us. I think she saw us. We'll let her sit there another five minutes and then bring her in."

"You'll let her sit there for ten minutes, Two."

"Yes sir. No problem sir. Can do. Two out."

"Yes sir, jumping sir. How high and tell me when I can come down." I said to Tuco when we were off the air. I really didn't give a flying fuck how long the woman sat out there so long as she didn't get shot. If the El Tee wanted to throw his weight around, let him. As Tuco and Skeeter always said, "It don't mean nothing."

I waved my hand at the woman, trying to reassure her. She knew where we were, but now she knew we saw her, and if she was patient she was going to be all right.

The El Tee was still on the horn, briefing the rest of Recon about Tuco and me and telling them to hold their position.

Then I got on. "Dragon One, this is Dragon Two."

"This is Dragon One. Go ahead two."

"Ask Preacher to send someone to brief my squad. I'm out here in limbo with my RTO."

"We'll take care of it Blondie."

"Thanks."

Tuco smirked. "You don't think we can trust the El Tee to do that, huh."

"No I don't. He thinks of every guy as only responsible to him. If they screw up, they deserve what happened. I think he's full of crap. Every man is responsible to himself, but all men are responsible for each other. Otherwise we're dead."

"Sometimes, I'm on his side," Tuco said. "It's easier. If it's his responsibility, it's also his fault."

"I know."

We settled in for our ten minute wait, eyes on the road in case anyone else showed up.

Maybe Tuco and I talked about this stuff more than we should, but we had to talk about it. Tuco wasn't very easy with authority. I'd heard the whole story and I knew why.

Everybody thought Tuco was a Latino guy from Texas. That's what he looked like. That's how he talked. He'd grown up with Chicanos. He let people think he was Chicano.

In Tuco's childhood home there were two flags, one Philippine and one American draped on opposite sides of the fireplace. There were photographs from the war, very few of his father, but several of Douglas MacArthur including a large blow up of his "return."

Tuco grew up knowing he'd join the Army. His father was grateful to the Army and convinced Tuco he owed the Army duty for his home and citizenship.

Of course no one had yet heard of Vietnam.

Tuco went to Junior College, studying bookkeeping. When he got his A.A. he joined up. The Army trained him as a finance clerk. In Nam he got assigned to Division's pay center.

I never got his story quite straight. Tuco hated garrison duty because there was too much "make work". He ticked off a couple of noncoms. He was sure they wrangled his transfer to the bush.

He was lucky to end up in my squad. I wasn't brown shoe army. I was a draftee, Sergeant only because I went to Shake 'N Bake school and earned my six stripes at Ft. Benning as a Non Commissioned Officer Candidate.

He thought the old guys screwed with him, and I had to prove I wasn't one of those guys. He could trust me; he could trust us. In the bush we were in a mess together and all we wanted was to keep each other alive.

For Recon he was a new guy even though he'd been in country a while. In Recon new guys always carried the radio or the gun unless someone else with more grunt time wanted to keep it. The radio telephone operator was always partnered with the squad leader. Tuco hadn't been to infantry training so I took him as RTO and taught him what he had to know.

The next new guy took the M-60. When the next new guy came Tuco kept his radio and our partnership. There's a rule in the bush; it's dumb to make friends. You never know what's going to happen. How will you feel if you have to pack him in a body bag? Well I'd feel it anyway. Tuco was my friend.

I'd swear we waited out there by the highway for fifteen minutes. Finally the radio squawked. "This is Dragon. Squads acknowledge."

"Dragon One"

"Dragon Two" Tuco said.

"Dragon Three"

"This is Dragon. Stand down your ambush. Get your food before it gets dark. Blondie you and Tuco can bring in your prisoner."

I wondered if he ever listened to any conversation he wasn't a part of. I grabbed the mike from Tuco. "Sir, please tell my squad we're coming in and remind them we've got a native."

"I'm taking care of it, Blondie. Don't mess yourself. I'll meet you at Skeeter's gun. Dragon out."

"Does he sound pissed to you?" I asked Tuco. I wasn't looking forward to our reception.

Tuco grinned. "Sometimes the only way out is through."

"Maybe not always," I said, and keyed the mike again.

"Sir, don't forget why I'm here. Ghost just showed up. I'll send in Tuco with the woman. Ghost can give me security while Tuco takes her in. I'll finish the Alpha Alpha. Dragon Two out."

"You're just pissing him off, amigo." Tuco said. "You have to come in sometime."

CHAPTER 21

I hooked up the Alpha Alpha in a few minutes. When I was done I asked Ghost to tell Tuco to send out the squad one at a time. Once Second Squad knew where the trip wire was, I passed the word for the other squads. It took almost an hour before everybody saw the trip with the crumpled cigarette package I'd dropped to mark it.

Meanwhile, Tuco and the squad took care of me. By the time I got back the old woman was as comfortable as possible. Tuco loaned her my poncho and a flat air mattress for a shelter. Somebody came up with a spare poncho liner.

Tuco and I would sleep out on his poncho. There was no hint of rain.

While I managed the Alpha Alpha, Tuco and the squad put more claymores out – not as booby traps but as command detonated mines. We could set them off remotely with a small hand generator called a clacker. If something did blow the Alpha the enemy might well sweep both sides of the road and come straight into us, but run into our claymores first.

Tuco also had been to the CP briefing. "They won't fly her out until morning because it's too close to dark." Tuco said. "Doc says she's stable and will make it. Tough as nails, he says."

"They're going for a sit down?" I asked. "We'll need an LZ."

163

I couldn't imagine swinging a Bronze Age wounded woman out on a jungle penetrator, and a hovering Medevac chopper could reveal the ambush.

"We've got one. First Squad went out on patrol. About four hundred meters down the highway there's a big clearing."

"Crops?"

"I didn't ask."

Doc had cleaned the woman's wound and taped a big dressing over it. Now she breathed more easily. She wasn't quiet though. Maybe Doc doped her for the pain, but it just loosened her up. She was still moaning some of the time, but like as not between moans she was jabbering away in the local language no one understood. She got quieter when Posthole brought her a nice hot C ration and a spoon. Maybe she'd go to sleep after dark.

Recon preferred quiet. We counted on it. We didn't carry flak jackets. We didn't wear helmets. We wore black berets to tell the VC who we were. According to Intel, our berets scared the crap out of them. We had snipers with us, but no mortar tubes. We didn't dig holes to sleep in at night like line companies. We never spoke above a whisper until the shooting started. We were stealthy and quiet, all in all a far better platoon than the El Tee deserved for his first command.

While Tuco heated water with heat tabs, I moved the radio to our left between our hootch and Posthole's. The radio needed to be in the middle of the squad to make it easy for the guys on watch to find it in the night. Each of us usually took an hour on watch with the last guy making up the difference. Tonight we'd do two hour shifts in pairs. The Colonel wanted us to double our security because the woman's wound was evidence Charley was in the neighborhood. I'd told the guys we'd just combine the adjacent watches. Tuco and I were on first.

The woman finished her food and began jabbering again. Several guys from the CP and Second Squad tried to get her quiet, but nothing worked.

Tuco heated a franks and beans C ration for himself. He'd made us both a cup of instant coffee since we were going to be awake for a couple of hours. My dinner was a beef and rice L.R.R.P. and a small can of fruit cocktail my Dad had sent.

I changed my socks. Tuco and I both put on a clean pair. We sloshed our dirty socks around in hot water with a little soap then rinsed with some cold and wrung them as dry as we could. The socks wouldn't dry tonight, but they would dry hanging from our packs tomorrow and become clean socks for tomorrow night.

Keeping your feet clean was important, and much easier if you had family help. Help was important. Dad sent me care packages with Desenex, Grape Kool Aid, WD-40, and fruit cocktail. I was pretty well off compared to some of the guys so I shared my stuff.

I took a walk through the squad to make sure everybody was okay and supplied for the night. A couple of guys complained about the woman's noise. I agreed it was a problem, but I told them I didn't know what we could do about it.

The El Tee was waiting with Ghost at my place when I got back. He was smoking a cigarette. There was still some light, but it was dim enough you could see the tip of it as an orange glow.

"Sir," I said, "With all due respect, a cigarette's not a good idea on ambush and certainly not at dusk. Charley can smell your smoke, sir, and if he sees the tip he can use it for a target."

He lifted an eyebrow, cupped the tip under his palm, took a deep drag and exhaled slowly on my poncho liner.

"With all due respect, huh? Fuckin' A. Maybe it's not a good idea Sergeant Blondie. Maybe it's a bad idea. Maybe I'm going to get fucking cancer some day. And my hootch won't stink of cigarette. Yours will. You are not my nanny, and let's agree for the moment I can pretty much do whatever I want, with all due respect."

"Yes sir. Of course, sir. What can we do for you sir?"

"Fucking mess this afternoon, wasn't it? Why didn't you guys grease the old woman? What's your story, Ghost?"

"She didn't look like a problem sir. I knew Tuco and Duvall could handle her. If she was walking point for a larger element, I could do much more damage after they passed."

"Tuco, what about you?"

"I could see she was unarmed, sir."

"Really? You knew she wasn't carrying a frag? Or a fucking pistol?"

"Not fuckin' likely," I said, trying to draw the heat off Tuco. "This woman's a primitive. She's barely covered by her clothes. One of her hands was tight to her wound, and the other hand visible and empty. She couldn't be carrying shit."

"I see you're big on fucking details, Blondie."

"Yes sir. I've been in Recon a long time. We're trained to observe and report, sir."

"Ah yes, the many fabled eight months, six months more than me. Perhaps I should listen to you more often."

"Of course that would be up to you, sir."

"Yes it would." He put out the cigarette. "So what's your plan now?"

"As you directed, sir. We're keeping a double watch. My gun's got a good position on the left end of Third's line. I've checked out everybody. We've got enough food, water, and ammo for tonight. I reminded them all to make up a log list for anything we need. I'm sure Rock will be asking for it in the next day or two."

"Sergeant Blondie, I don't think that's going to deal with your problem."

"Sir?"

"All that fucking moaning and jabber behind you. Don't you think she's going to draw some attention?"

"Not a lot I can do about it sir."

"You gotta, Blondie. Think of something. You brought in the fucking problem. You've got to fix it or you're going to be fucked.

"Yes sir. What' you got in mind, sir."

"Not a damned thing, Sergeant. Not a damned thing. It ain't my fucking problem, not my problem or Ghost's problem."

"Sir?"

"You wouldn't have this problem if Tuco'd greased her like he should. You wouldn't have this problem if she'd walked into the ambush. You've got this problem because she stopped on the road."

"Yes sir. She stopped sir. She knew where I was."

"Did you wave at her?"

"No sir," Tuco said. "You didn't order that sir. You wanted her to walk through the ambush. Of course we didn't wave at first."

"I didn't until after she saw us and stopped," I said, "but I've gotta tell you I thought about it."

"I'll bet you fucking did," the El Tee said. "Never mind. I won't bust you for what you're thinking. I don't care what you think. I care what you do. Right now you've got to do something about this noisy old woman."

"Sir, we're doing our best. She's been housed, fed, and medicated. She'll fall asleep soon sir. She'll be all right."

"Maybe not," the El Tee said. "Think about it. Think she's going to sleep if the shooting starts? Think she's going to be quiet then? Don't you think she'll give Sir Charles a good idea of where you're at? In case you haven't noticed, she's right next to you."

"Do you have an idea, sir?" Tuco asked.

"I told you, soldier. This isn't my problem. Tonight I couldn't give a damn if you fellas get fucked. I can only think of one damn thing. It's a sin so I can't do it, and I can't order it."

I could see it coming, but Tuco didn't. "What's that sir?" He asked.

"Either of you boys Catholic?" the El Tee asked.

"No sir."

"No sir."

Tuco was lying to follow my lead. When was the last time you met a Filipino who wasn't Catholic?

"Well that's good," the El Tee said. "I'm Catholic. If I was to do the old woman, it would be a mortal sin. You boys don't have that problem. If trouble starts just slip her a bullet and who will be the wiser?"

Night had fallen. We couldn't see the El Tee's face. We could hear him as he stumbled away in the dark towards the C.P.

"Come on," I said to Tuco grabbing my ammo bag and my M-16. "We're on watch."

We made our way through the short distance in the dark to the squad radio. Ghost followed. I wasn't completely cool with that, but like I said nobody really told Ghost what to do. Near the radio we could hear it. Pete at the CP was checking in each squad and we could hear the burst of static that started each call when he keyed his mike.

"CP this is Dragon Two"

"Dragon Two, Roger. Glad you could make it."

"The El Tee was telling us how to strengthen our position. He should be stumbling in there pretty soon. Two Out."

"What are we going to do?" Tuco asked when he was sure the mike wasn't open.

"Nothing to do," I said. "He's just being a fucking ROTC asshole."

Most of the ROTC officers were okay, but often it seemed as if many of the bad officers like the El Tee were ROTC graduates. The OCS guys were all cool. The West Pointers were outstanding. There were only a few of the best kind, guys who made their way up ranks as noncoms going on to OCS or to getting commissioned direct. The Colonel was one of those, a highly decorated Ranger during the Korean War commissioned from the ranks.

"You know he wants us to do it," Tuco said.

"No I don't. He's just fucking with our heads. He can't order it."

"Why not?"

Tuco was squirrelly about authority. He'd been fucked with too much at Division rear. Once he told me he never felt safe until he got out with Recon but before the El Tee came to our platoon.

"He can't. He can't order a murder. Once we proved she was a civilian, he can't order us to shoot."

"It's a free fire zone."

"Even those aren't free," I said. "That just means the El Tee can order a shoot without checking with the Colonel. He still can't do anything illegal. Otherwise he'd no longer be an officer or a gentleman."

"But he wants us to," Tuco said. "Otherwise why tell us?"

"To fuck with our heads. You heard the man. He don't give a shit what happens to us. We can be fucked for all he cares. He thinks we should kill the old woman, but he's too chicken shit to do it himself. He's a fucking disgrace. I just hope he's a good enough politician with the Colonel to get assigned somewhere else."

"But is he right?" Tuco asked. "Won't she screw us up like he said? You know she'll be screaming if the shit starts to fly."

"She won't be the only one," I said. "If it happens tonight we're going to need to yell to each other just to make sure none of us get shot by accident."

"I could help you out," Ghost said. "I could do her and nobody would see it. I mean since it's such a problem for the two of you. It don't mean nothing to me."

Now I knew why he was there.

"Leave her alone," Tuco said. "We got this. This is Second Squad business. We can handle it. You're on the ambush line with Third. You've got a job."

"Fine. Your call," Ghost said.

"It's not a problem," I said. "You think it's likely this is a real NVA probe? You know how quiet it's been since last June in Cambodia. We've only made contact half a dozen times, and never anything big. You think they're sending in a big armed force? Kissinger's in fucking Paris. They're just going to wait us out."

"We'll be all right," Tuco said.

"Of course we'll be," I said. "We won't do anything stupid. None of us wants to be the last guy shot."

"But if they do hit us tonight?" Tuco asked.

We were sitting cross legged on the ground. I reached over, found his shoulder. "When the time comes we'll do what we have to. We always do," I said. "Now's not the time to worry about it."

After a while I heard Posthole start to snore. A grunt can sleep anywhere, sometimes even standing up. Most of the guys were sleeping on the ground, but over in First Squad there was a guy in a hammock and one of my guys was sleeping in a bright green tube tent someone mailed from home.

Real darkness can seem to be safe. With a canopy of jungle overhead, you can't see a damn thing, but no damn thing can see you either.

We felt safe. The night was at the low edge of warm and the air humid. Since we couldn't see anything we might as well be sitting out some spring night on a back porch in Indiana.

Ghost was still with us. I don't know why he didn't go home to Third, but as far I was concerned that was his business.

We fell to talking about plans for when we were "back in the world," a phrase that meant going home to the U.S. "Back in the world" was an alien place. We had vivid memories, but we all knew it was a very long ways in time and distance from the jungle we were in.

"Amigo, I don't think I can ever go home to Texas," Tuco said. "I don't think I could tell my father how this is all screwed up; I don't think I could not tell him. Maybe I'll just buy a Harley and visit every other state."

Most of our pay was being held by the Army. For single guys in the bush like us all we could spend it on was beer. Skeeter managed the beer collection. At company headquarters in Phouc Vinh the supply guys bought it for us and shipped it out with our resupply. We could not carry or drink enough beer to make much dent in our pay. Old timers like Tuco and me both saved up a few thousand bucks.

I told Tuco my personal fantasy. "I want to buy a mountain top where there aren't any roads. Maybe I'll buy some concertina wire and fence the place. Maybe I just won't tell anybody where I am. I'll make my own sawmill, build a cabin in the woods, and live off the land. No other people. Nothing."

"No women?" Tuco asked.

"Well they can come if they want."

Tuco giggled inaudibly in the dark.

"Or maybe I could buy me a trailer park with some nice women already in it," I said.

Tuco giggled again. "What about you, Ghost?"

"Trailer park's as good an idea as any," Ghost said. "What difference does it make?"

The radio squawked. "Dragon Two this, is CP"

"CP go ahead."

"Dragon Two the El Tee says to pipe down. You guys are having too much fun. This is supposed to be an ambush."

"CP isn't Dragon asleep?"

"No I'm not asleep. Pipe down."

"Dragon Two, Roger."

We weren't safe from the El Tee even in the dark. The radio call probably made Tuco think about it again.

"You think he really wants us to kill her, Blondie?"

"Tuco we don't care what he wants. We care about doing what we have to. We care about getting everybody back to the world."

He didn't say anything more about it. Ghost left and went back to Third. After a few minutes Posthole showed up with Raspberry to take the next watch.

CHAPTER 22

The Alpha blew at 3:06 by my watch.

Behind us the woman screamed and then a torrent of talk, unintelligible but clearly panicked.

Grabbing my ammo bag and 16, I groped toward the radio. Tuco stayed behind to hold our position.

There was no one on the radio. Ace and Chico knew I'd be coming so they'd already left for their position.

The radio squawked. "This is Dragon. Roll Call."

The radio squawked unreadably; two squads had tried to speak at once.

"Dragon Two," I said.

"Dragon Three"

"One"

"This is Dragon. You're not in holes. You've got no cover. Muzzle flash will give away your position. Nobody shoots without a clear target. Use your claymores or grenades. Cut down the hootches. Get all your ponchos on the ground. Cut down that damned hammock; I don't want to see that damned tube tent in the morning."

The squads acknowledged.

I moved up to the closest hootch and said, "Rogers."

"Rangers," said a whispered voice.

This was our pass phrase, a challenge with response. We didn't think Asians could pronounce the letter R, though Alphabet who was part Japanese had no trouble.

"Pass the word to the left," I said to Posthole and Raspberry. "Don't fire a weapon unless you've got a clear target. Use your claymores or frags on things you can't see. Ground the ponchos and the tube tent." I didn't bother to tell them to keep quiet. They didn't need telling. The loudest sound I could hear was the beat of my heart despite the screams of the woman.

I picked up the Prick 25 and moved right. When my challenge was finally acknowledged at the edge of my own tarp, I slid quietly down on my poncho liner next to Tuco.

"Anything moving?"

"Nothing. Maybe shifting bamboo."

You might think we'd hear them first. Our hootch was closest to the tripwire.

"Slide over and tell Alphabet and Skeeter. Don't shoot the M60 at all unless there's an all out assault. No other shooting if they don't see a clear target. Otherwise frags. If they've still got a roof on their hootch tell them to cut it down."

The woman was sobbing now.

The gun team couldn't put a claymore out because our target road was to their front. A claymore out there on the road couldn't be easily concealed.

For a moment I was truly alone in the dark and trying not to be afraid.

The jungle is never completely quiet. Leaves shift in the wind. There are animals, many very loud, like the lizard whose cry sounded just like "Fuck You".

In the blackness you can see little more than nothing. Where you can see it, the sky is faintly lighter. From a very low angle you may see a hint of a silhouette, at best our "clear target."

Meanwhile you listen. Ignore the woman. Listen.

Most noise will not be the enemy, but you listened for any metallic click, any breaking branch or twig. You try to hear the pattern. We taped the metal of our gear to keep it quiet. Charley taped his too.

Tuco was taking his time. Maybe he was chatting up Alphabet. This was the kind of situation when it was too easy for 'Bet to panic.

Fear makes fools of us all. In the jungle dark it's always better to stay and fight than run. There's nowhere to run in the dark. Standing up would be the first mistake. On the ground you're practically invisible; standing you were a silhouette against barely lighter sky. If you ran in the dark you could not be distinguished from the enemy. You were noisy. You broke twigs; your metal rattled. Charley wouldn't have to shoot you if your friends did.

Better to wait; at night fight was always better than flight.

When the El Tee first said NVA I thought he was full of shit. Now I knew I could be wrong. The old woman came to us with a hole in her side. Somebody put it there. With the report the El Tee had from intel, like as not it was the VC or the NVA. They abused or ignored the Montagnards just as we did.

Something had stepped on the Alpha Alpha, likely someone following the old woman's trail or ours.

Maybe it was better at night. Anyone moving at night was more than likely a bad guy. During the nighttime they were no better than us, though they might outnumber us. During the daytimes, they might drive the Montagnards in front as a screen to flush us out. Shooting at night there were no innocents to hit.

And I had to shut up. I had to quiet my fucking hippy college kid imagination. I didn't need to hear myself think. I needed to listen. I needed to be very still. I needed...

I needed not to think I was in the horror movie where the music turns up and the killer appears with a machete for the girl. At the movies I could leave the theater. I could not leave the place where I was now.

"Rogers."

"Rangers" I said.

Tuco slid in beside me.

"How are they holding up?"

"It's good that Alphabet is with Skeeter. They'll be fine."

That was huge for me. I trusted Tuco's judgment over most. The gun was as solid as I could make it, more than solid because we were guarding it on the left.

"Slide back and try to quiet the woman," I said

After a minute she was quieter, only muffled sobs.

"Rogers"

"Rangers"

"I don't know if I comforted her or scared her," Tuco said. "Anyway. Mostly she's shut up."

Now all we could do was wait.

I was no longer alone. The night again became a warm, soft blanket.

"Blondie if you want to sleep, I can't."

"Are you kidding, Tuco? Me neither."

I tried to think about the enemy. How would it be for them?

They're walking down a road under the cover of darkness. Suddenly there is an explosion. Many should be dead and several wounded. They guess about us as we guessed about them.

We might be right there, beside them in the dark. We might be watching. How large a force are we? They wonder. Where are we? How are we positioned?

If they were large enough, they probe. If they were too small they run away but mark where we were.

And we still wait.

"Dragon, this is Dragon One"

"Go One"

"We've got movement, Dragon."

"Describe."

"Many feet. Muffled sound. Maybe as much as a hundred meters the other side of us. If they're on the road they have us surrounded. If they're not on the road we've been flanked."

"Dragon, this is Three"

"Go Three."

"I've got light enough on the road. They're not here."

"Stand by. Dragon out"

I put my hand on Tuco's wrist.

"Hold the fort, buddy." I said. "I've got to check our left." I took the radio.

Posthole and his hootchmate were fine. They had heard nothing.

Recon was fat right now; we had thirty five men, but in Second Squad I only had eight. I kept going left. I hadn't been down this far since dusk so I almost tripped over them.

"Rogers" came the whisper in the dark.

"Rangers. It's me, Blondie. Can you hear them?"

"Sure. Be quiet. Listen for yourself," Ace said.

I listened a few seconds before I heard it, apparently quite far out. Sound travels better at night, but I could only guess the distance, more than fifty meters at the least.

These men were not moving quietly. They seemed not to care if anyone heard. There were muffled sounds and grunts, voices surely spoken above a whisper with no regard for us.

If we were very lucky, they might pass us in the dark.

I gave Ace and Chico four of my M-16 magazines. "You're closer," I said. "You may need these more than I do."

I still had plenty.

We weren't going to be lucky. As I moved slowly back toward Posthole and Raspberry, I could hear the gooks moving closer. I was almost to their position when a single shot rang out, the sharp crack of an M-16.

"Got him!" rang out a voice from somewhere in First Squad.

The woman screamed again.

I hit the ground and rolled over to face the outside of the perimeter between the two positions.

There were many explosions, and a couple of shots, most of them behind me near First Squad, guys using frags and claymores.

I spoke out loud for the first time in days, "Raspberry and Posthole. This is Blondie I'm on your left and maybe rear moving toward you." No sense being quiet anymore, they knew we were here.

"Over here," Post called

There were screams among the enemy, and chaos of trampling and breaking sounds out in the bamboo. There might be hundreds of them. I crept toward Posthole's position.

The El Tee got on the horn, speaking out loud to make sure the battalion heard him.

"Enterprise this is Dragon."

I heard Prick 25 squawk when they acknowledged but I couldn't hear the words. They were on the battalion freq. I could hear the word if I switched over but there really was no point.

"This is Dragon," the El Tee said. "We have contact. Large force. Company size at the least. These are my co-ordinates." He rattled off numbers. "Request fire support."

"You call it in, Rock," he told the Platoon Sergeant. "I'll be out on the line with the men."

It wasn't exactly quiet; we could hear squeals or screams in the bamboo, but nothing close. For a couple of minutes there was nothing else but the sound of Rock and the first test rounds of artillery. Suddenly there were more grenade explosions, claymores, explosions, and more gunfire, some of it close. I was pretty sure Posthole had blown a claymore. I thought the enemy had closed up on us to avoid the hell coming next. Artillery wasn't allowed to fire too close.

"Fire for effect." Rock said, and then we could all hear the One Five Five rounds screaming in like freight trains, carpeting the bamboo with explosions, rocking the earth.

Over the artillery we shouted challenge and response.

"You guys okay?" I asked, rolling into Posthole's position.

"Yeah. We blew one to hell."

"You need anything? I gotta get back to Tuco," I said.

Rock was still on the radio adjusting Artillery.

"We're fine, Posthole said, "But tell me, Blondie. Why the hell aren't they shooting back?"

"I've got no fucking idea."

We all jammed ourselves flat as the next salvo of One Five Five slammed in to our front.

I moved out as soon as it was over.

Once again we shouted challenge and response and at last I was back at my own poncho.

Tuco was pretty shook up. I couldn't see him, but I could feel him trembling. I found his arm in the dark and squeezed.

"Relax." I said. "You're not alone anymore, and I'm not going anywhere. Everyone's got what they need. We just got to tough this out."

I didn't check on Alphabet and Skeeter. They were better armed than anybody else with the twelve belts of M-60 ammo the squad had carried.

The artillery had stopped. Squawks on the El Tee's Prick 25 continued with no voices on mine. The El Tee was back on it talking. I heard the choppers overhead.

"This is Dragon. Check in"

I waited for the other squad leaders before I called in with "Dragon Two."

"This is Dragon. We have Cobras on station. Get everybody as concealed as possible. I need to show them a light."

"You can start praying now, Tuco. I'd appreciate it. I'll be back in a minute."

I crouched and ran. There were still no incoming rounds.

"Rogers"

"Rangers"

"Posthole, cover up and pass the word. The El Tee's flashing a strobe for Cobras."

I ran back to Tuco. "Tell Skeeter and Alphabet to cover up."

Tuco also ran and was back in less than a minute. We shoved our packs well away from ourselves, pulled in the edge of the poncho we were using as a ground cloth and huddled under our poncho liners. They were camouflaged.

"Dragon this is Dragon Two" I whispered. "We're concealed." We weren't under cover. The poncho liners weren't going to stop bullets.

"Roger Two," the El Tee said.

Mysteriously there were still no discernible shots fired by the enemy, no new explosions. The jungle was still alive with sound, but it became more difficult to be sure of the enemy. The One Five Five rounds had broken trees and bamboo. Leaves were shaken, and broken trunks moaned and snapped as they fell. I still thought I could hear movement but now it was more difficult to tell.

After the other squads checked in, I glanced back at the CP. The El Tee must be lying prone. In the strobe light I could see only his hand holding the plastic case as the light blinked. It was only about three feet off the ground. I guessed he was prone beneath the hand.

A long minute passed and the hand was still there.

The El Tee's Prick 25 squawked again.

"Fuck," he said, loud and mad.

The light went out. When the light and hand appeared again they were almost eight feet off the ground. He was standing up, a damn gutsy move holding a bright blinking light in the night, a fine target.

The El Tee's radio squawked again and the light went out. I couldn't make out individual words, but I could still hear the distinctive rhythmic distortion the interference on the choppers made of the human voice. He had a Cobra pilot on the horn.

A Willy Pete round burst brightly in the bamboo among the enemy.

"Fire for effect," the El Tee said out loud. We could hear the electric "Brrrapp" from their Gatling guns, and the whoosh and bang of their rockets slamming into the earth and jungle more near to us than the One Five Five's ever could.

Still there was no incoming fire from the enemy. We had shot at least one if not several. We had thrown grenades and blown claymores. We had hurled lead and exploded steel at them. Listen as we might for the pop-pop-pop sound of an AK-47, there was none.

Maybe we had killed them all. Maybe they had run around us in the jungle through the dark.

Maybe, I began to fear, nothing.

My radio squawked again.

"We're getting no incoming fire," the El Tee said. "Battalion says if we're taking no hits, we should wait until light so we can see what we've got."

Branches fell, twigs snapped, and leaves shook. The jungle was alive with sound, but none of the screams, grunts, and squeals we had heard before.

No one slept. When there was light enough, I could easily move between the positions of the squad and make sure everyone was okay. Soon there was light enough to see our kills.

Slowly we begin to move about and count. The first had taken but few steps away from Arkansas, the guy who fired the first round of M-16. Arkansas's bullet had gone in right under the shoulder, piercing the heart, a perfect shot for a fine barbecue.

All in all we had killed fifteen wild pigs.

Ghost ran whooping among the carcasses dabbing his face with pig blood; Sharkey, his squad leader, ran after him to get him quiet.

I ran out toward what was left of my Alpha Alpha as soon as I could. The claymore's were gone, all six blown. The trigger still tested good, and the battery still had juice.

There were no bodies, no NVA or VC, and not even pig. There was a fine long carpet of iridescent blue feathers carpeting dirt road for more than a hundred meters. Never before or since have I seen anything remotely like it. I couldn't imagine what bird it could be. There were so many feathers. How large could it be? Or perhaps there had been many close in a flock when one had stepped or flown into the trigger.

Still there were no bodies for even one bird, just the vivid carpet of blue green feathers and down.

Back inside the perimeter I found Tuco shirtless, M-16 dangling from his hand, crying, standing over the lifeless body of the old woman. She had been shot in the head.

The El Tee was talking out loud on the horn to battalion. "Negative Negative," he said. "I can't count the human blood trails. They're indistinguishable from pig. We do have a casualty. The old woman's dead. They were here. They had to be shooting to kill her. We just didn't hear it. They must have taken their bodies out when they left."

I didn't think there had been incoming gunfire. I don't think anyone else thought so either, but none of us said anything. No one was better than the El Tee for inventing the politic lie. We might never know what bodies battalion reported to Division. None of us cared.

Four hundred meters down the road we secured the LZ. A chopper came down and took the body of the woman. If Tuco had shot her the day before, we'd have left her in the jungle. Shot in perimeter she was our ally, and we would honor her as one of our own.

We moved a couple of thousand meters and took a break. The El Tee had been talking to the Colonel. He had us set up a temporary perimeter and asked the squad leaders to join him in the C.P.

"Gentlemen, this is still an ambush. We're not done yet. This highway is still our target. The wise men still think the NVA is on the move. They think maybe the old woman was running from them.

"I'll be walking with First Squad on point looking for another good place to set up. I want something thicker than bamboo if I can find it. The men need rest after last night. I'd like to stop early if we can."

We moved five clicks further to the west and set up the ambush on the road again.

I had the Alpha Alpha again. The trigger, wiring and battery were still good. With spare det cord and claymores, one each from each squad, I made a string of three. I had it all set up, but didn't put out the trip wire or connect it. It was only about one o'clock and we had many hours to wait until dusk.

This time about 14:30 hours we got something.

At first there was a distant muffled sound, rhythmic and low, "Hooo Haaaw; Hooo Haaaw." There was nothing visible from Second Squad's position to the next turn of the road, but we knocked down everything that stuck up and took firing positions.

Montangnards appeared at a distant bend. An old man led them. They carried sticks impaled with paper they thrust into the air as they walked and chanted.

"Chieu Hoi; Chieu Hoi; Cheiu Hoi"

We could guess what the papers were. Psyops sent choppers with loudspeakers through the night telling Vietnamese ghost stories and strewing Chieu Hoi propaganda everywhere. Sometimes where we walked there seemed to be thousands of leaflets everywhere, half page advertisements for the "Open Arms" program.

Tired of fighting or living in a free fire zone? Just surrender to American or South Vietnamese forces, all will be forgiven and we'll find you a new home.

These people looked tired. All were barefoot and clothed in little more the rags. There seemed to be a great many. They filled the road completely side to side, six to eight at a time, all chanting, all swinging their sticks.

I had left Tuco at our position and moved up on Skeeter's gun. I wanted his shots to be selective.

"Are they trying to surrender?" Alphabet asked in a loud whisper.

"Damned if I know," I said.

"It don't mean nothing." Skeeter said, staring down the barrel of the M-60. "Ghost's on our right."

Alphabet and I knew what he meant. If the 'yards were alone we could let them surrender. If they had VC or NVA Company driving them from behind as a screen we still had a fight and some of these Stone Age people would get in the way. Even if there were no bad guys, Ghost or some other jerked trigger could start a slaughter.

I hated the ambush yesterday with the woman. I hated this one today. If we fired even a shot, the Montagnards would scatter, but at least they might not be killed. The El Tee wasn't shooting. He was letting them walk through so we could ambush the VC or the NVA if they were among them, driving them.

Kissinger was in fucking Paris, but we were here.

They kept coming. I tried to count. I lost track somewhere above a hundred and thirty and still saw no guns.

But how could we know? Their guns would shoot only at a target. And who was going to volunteer to be one? I wouldn't order it, but the El Tee might. Meanwhile with every step they took the Montagnards moved quickly to an all but certain doom.

We were certain of nothing but our fear. Someone in the platoon might break. Someone might shoot. If any of us fired, most of us would. We needed to know if there were guns. We needed to know if there were none.

Maybe we'd know only if I stepped into the road, but I couldn't do it, my life was still worth more to me than theirs.

But how could I live the life I'd have left after we had killed them?

A lone figure stepped onto the road just five meters from Skeeter, Alphabet, and me. Despite dirt and dark skin, Tuco paled before the advancing men. Lowering his M-16 he said, "Chieu Hoi."

Screams and chaos. Some 'Yards ran toward Tuco, others ran away. The chanting resumed and became more intense. Tuco was mobbed with people.

I ran to Tuco, Skeeter and Alphabet close behind. My M-16 was pointed at the ground. There were no shots fired. There was no enemy. Once more we were fighting only fear.

Recon's Third Squad stepped onto the trail and followed me.

It was difficult to reach Tuco. He was surrounded by a mob. He was smiling through tears by the time I reached him. So was I. I could hear the CP radio squawking behind me; the El Tee was talking to battalion.

I embraced Tuco and thumped him in the back with my M-16. "Damn brother. Next time don't do that."

"Blondie there ain't never going to be no next time."

Rock, booming loudly in English the people couldn't understand, gestured broadly with his hands and began to marshal them into a line, while shouting orders to us.

"Get your gear. Five minutes. Third Squad point. Second Squad, left flank security on the column of our guests. First Squad right flank security."

Shortly we were escorting our stone age brothers and sisters into the twentieth century. After a couple of clicks we secured a large clearing on a crossroads. Flights of helicopters arrived. The Colonel's bird was first. He shook the El Tee's hand. Shortly the chieftain who had led these people through the valley of the shadow was urging on his flock. Until now all they could know of helicopters was death; now they scrambled into the waiting birds.

We were loading helicopters for more than an hour. Rock detailed Alphabet to keep a careful count. His count was a hundred and sixteen. Many ran back into the jungle with fear. By the time the Chief got on the last helicopter a translator had confirmed some were gone. At least this piece of the Chief's tribe would have new life less certain of sudden death.

We were exhausted physically and emotionally by the time the last bird left. The El Tee didn't make us walk far. We resumed the ambush in our last position and once more secured ourselves for the night.

The Colonel ordered us back to the Firebase the next morning. We had a little job to finish first. We humped back very carefully over our own trail to the site of our war with the pigs and collected the bodies. The Colonel's bird flew out all of them. It took about three trips of stacked dead porkers on the floor of his bird.

A flight of Huey's came to pull us out. As always I was damned glad to go. A forward firebase might be the front line for the cooks and headquarters types at Phouc Vinh, but for me it was vacation in the rear. I could shower with water sun warmed in a tank. I could sleep under a roof, though it was only half a round of sewer culvert covered with sandbags.

There were more than enough pigs to feed our battalion, and we gave the rest to the Cobra flights who served us. The pilots tried to claim credit for all of the kills so we gave them five pigs and told them that was half.

Echo Company got fat on barbecue. All evening long the men from artillery and Bravo Company came to thank us for the feast.

I didn't have much appetite myself. I noticed Tuco didn't either. I let him alone. He had to live with his own conscience, and I couldn't imagine how I could be much help.

I wasn't at all surprised when Ace showed up with Skeeter and Posthole.

"Blondie, we've got to talk."

"Go ahead," I said.

"We want to know what's going to happen," he said. "We want to know what you're going to do."

I played dumb. "I don't know," I said. "I don't know what I'm going to do. Why don't I ask you what you're going to do? It don't mean nothing."

"Fuck your noise," said Ace. "What we're going to do don't mean nothing. We're not the leaders here. You were dumb enough to take the squad. It matters what you think and what you do because we're going to follow."

"I've got nothing in mind," I said.

"Don't you think you should?" Skeeter said. "We compared notes. The guys in the CP blabbed. They told us what the El Tee said. We know the choice you had, and better still we all know where we were on the night of the pigs. Each of us was teamed with somebody else and didn't leave them. We were never alone in the dark. I was with Alphabet."

"I was with Raspberry."

"I was with Chico."

"You were everywhere. Only you and Tuco were ever alone."

I searched their faces. I still wasn't sure what they wanted to do.

"Spell it out for me," I said. "Maybe I'm too thick between the ears."

Skeeter sighed. "An old woman got skragged," he said. "None of us think you could do it. We know what the El Tee said. He said it was our problem. Nobody else could do it but Tuco or you."

"And you want...?"

"We want you to tell us what you're going to do."

"Maybe it was Ghost," I said. "He volunteered to do it, but Tuco told him we could handle it."

"Maybe it was Tuco," Skeeter said. "I checked on Ghost. For once he was following orders. The woman screamed at the beginning of the ambush and Ghost never left Farley until dawn."

My turn to sigh. "Listen," I said. "It don't mean nothing. The El Tee told battalion we took incoming rounds. Battalion believes it. Battalion would like to believe we killed fifteen more who weren't pigs. Nobody's asking questions.

"Besides, you don't know nothing. Maybe I did kill her. Maybe some one of you did and is lying with his partner. Hell, maybe the El Tee crawled out of the CP and did it himself. You don't know nothing. All you can do is guess."

"But I do guess," Posthole said. "And what if somebody asks?"

"What if they do," I said. "Don't you think they're going to ask me first? If I killed her I'm not going to tell you. I'm not going to tell them, and I'm not going to tell them they should guess it was Tuco.

"Another thing," I said. "If I were you, I wouldn't ask Tuco. You can think what you like. Maybe you shouldn't ask him because he'll tell you it was me. Or maybe you shouldn't ask him because you really don't want to know the answer. Knowing will make it harder not to tell. None of us want to know. I won't ask him either. I promise."

Maybe some guys wouldn't have said that. I had more or less told them that Tuco was the one. I didn't think that mattered. Our military occupational specialty is operations and intelligence. These guys knew the difference between knowing and suspecting. I wanted to get it. It was important not know. None of them would have to lie about it.

I looked around again and felt a lot better. Skeeter was grinning now. Ace had lit a cigarette and was savoring it. I knew we were on the same page.

"This is Second Squad," I said. "We take care of each other unless and until we die. As long as I'm in charge we're going to keep on doing it."

Skeeter was still grinning. "That's what we thought you'd say," he said.

"Come on. Let's get some more pig."

I didn't want pig.

I wish I could say I knew what to expect. I wasn't thinking too far ahead, just a minute, maybe an hour, or rarely into the next day. I lived only in the now. My first and only job was to get us all home. I had no regard for what happened after. Fucking Kissinger was in Paris, I was still in the bush.

We were four days on the firebase. Recon welcomed the rest, at least for the most part. Second Squad was out on night ambush once, and afterward I was grateful. We were still the same team. Guys did their jobs. Nobody gave Tuco a second glance unless they needed him, and when they needed him they counted on him as if nothing had happened.

I still worried about Tuco. I alone of the squad was really sure he'd killed her. The others were right to suspect the two of us. Only I knew I didn't do it and knew he did, and I couldn't ask what it meant to him.

After a while I didn't mind so much. He didn't kill her for the El Tee; he killed her for us. He was wrong because there was no enemy, but he didn't know. He killed her because he had to, because otherwise he could not believe we would be safe.

Maybe he regretted it later. Maybe he threw himself before the Montagnards to make up for it. Had the enemy been there he'd have paid with his life. Since the enemy was not, perhaps he felt he bought back her death with the many Montagnard lives he'd saved.

Gradually, I stopped worrying about Tuco, and began to worry about myself. I managed not to count when I realized I only had three months left, but I began to worry I might not make it.

I never put myself before anyone else in the squad. There were only two guys, Tuco and Skeeter, who did not walk point, because they carried our most valuable assets, the Prick 25 and the gun.

One day when it was my turn I passed a chicom claymore and did not see it. When the gooks blew it, Raspberry was killed. Everyone else had at least a ding, but Tuco was bad off. Parts of the Prick 25 were deep in his belly. At least he was alive, though we were making him hold onto his own guts when we loaded him on the chopper.

"Choose to live you fucking asshole," I said. "Choose to live and I will find you and keep you safe when we get home."

He was alive when he left, but I was terrified and all but certain I'd never see him again.

The El Tee was surprisingly cool about it. I expected to get an earful about my oversight, but got something else.

He grinned at me. "Tough, Blondie. Nobody's perfect. I guess you're no longer a virgin."

"He doesn't look like he's going to make it," I said.

"Maybe not," the El Tee said. "But don't go worrying about it like a hippy college kid. Hope for the best. Expect the worst, and close the door on it. You still gotta live. And we still need you wide awake and ready to rock and roll."

I knew he was right. There'd be other shoot outs, and I was still here.

I got a note from Tuco a little more than a month before I was due back in the world.

"Dear Sergeant Asshole," it began. "I guess I've made it in spite of your screw up. I crap in a bag now, but I'm really okay. Come and see me when you get home."

The return address was Letterman Army Hospital, Presidio of San Francisco.

We were in the bush. The mail had been kicked out of the supply chopper with our rations and a block of ice in a bag that shattered. I sat still for quite a while, but I let Skeeter read the letter and he passed it around the platoon. It was supposed to be good news. Of course it was good news. Tuco was okay, except he crapped through a hole in his side.

So why didn't I feel good about it? What did I feel?

Some of the guys made a point of telling me they were glad he was okay. I wouldn't say they were congratulating me. I hadn't done anything. I hadn't spotted the damn mine. If he'd died, it would have been my fault. I got no credit for his life.

Again I expected the El Tee might rub it in; congratulations Tuco's alive. He said nothing. It was casual news to him. Tuco alive or dead was all the same, which I suppose was true. We weren't getting him back.

I wasn't celebrating either. What could I feel? Nothing would be the same again. Tuco would always crap in a bag. Raspberry would always be dead. There would be no trailer park. I would not build a mountain retreat. There was no place I could go to get away from here.

I had endured almost my whole year in Vietnam, and seemed suddenly to lose my nerve. I wasn't frightened, but I became too cautious. I was a danger to the squad who needed confidence in their leadership. I talked to Skeeter, and we went to the El Tee. For once he listened. We reorganized.

Skeeter gave the M-60 to Alphabet. Newby Ryan partnered up with Alphabet. Skeeter took the radio. I spent the last month doing my best to teach Skeeter what it meant to be the squad leader.

"Leave no man behind" one of our slogans said. I had given myself to Recon for a whole year but now I'd leave them, probably abandon them forever. Reorganizing the squad to put Skeeter in charge was the last best thing I could do.

A month later I caught a flight back to the world, and a future I could not imagine.

CHAPTER 23

May 22,2006

"Thank you," Lily said. "I always wanted to know what it was like and none of your other war stories told the truth. Have you ever told this before?"

"No. Never."

"How do you feel?"

"Tired. Spent. Scared. I feel empty, hollowed out."

"You've carried that story a long time," Lily said finally.

"Like a heavy pack," I said. "When you drop it off your shoulders you almost seem to float. But maybe I didn't carry it; maybe it carried me.

"What's that supposed to mean?"

"I always wondered how Tuco could live with the guilt. I always worried that one day he wouldn't. There would be trouble, and I would have to deal with it. Sometimes I don't think it's an accident I became a cop."

She nodded. "You're all about control," she said. "You're afraid to lose it. You have one nightmare, wake up choking me, and instantly move out."

"I've had many nightmares," I said. "And Tuco's in most of them. I'm sure he has them too."

"Did you ever talk about the woman's death. Did you ever ask him if he did it?"

"No. Never did. I wasn't curious. I didn't need to ask. I didn't want to ask because I knew what the answer would be. If I didn't kill her, only he could, but so long as he didn't tell me I didn't have to do anything about it. I didn't ask then and I haven't asked since."

"What would you have to do?"

"Well tell somebody, I guess. Aren't you supposed to when someone confesses to a murder?"

"Who would you have told?"

"The Colonel probably. I couldn't trust what the El Tee might do because he wouldn't want to be caught out for the cover up."

"Maybe he wouldn't think it was a murder.," she said.
"Maybe he'd think it was, what-you-call-it, an operational necessity.."

"Oh it was murder all right because it wasn't necessary. Nobody was shooting at us."

"You don't need to shout," she said.

"Sorry."

"You really don't know what the Colonel would have done," she said.

"I suppose he would have launched some formal process, an inquiry of some kind, an investigation to determine if discipline was required. He wouldn't let the whole weight of it fall on him."

"So why didn't you tell him? She asked. "You had suspicions and suppositions. Why should all the weight fall on you?"

"You really don't get it," I said. "I wasn't any more loyal to the Colonel than I was loyal to the El Tee. I had to do what they told me, but I had bigger responsibility than all that, bigger than playing tattle tale on my friend."

"Please don't shout," she said.

"Sorry." I took a deep breath and tried to calm down. "I was a draftee, not a volunteer, but I had accepted the responsibility. We weren't over there trying to win a war. Fucking Kissinger was in Paris trying to make a peace. My job was taking care of my men. I was loyal to them far more than I was to the war machine.

"It was my job to try to get everybody home in one piece. And that included Tuco. I couldn't tell the Colonel or anybody and risk the chance they might think he was guilty too and lock him up or kill him."

"He was your friend," she said gently. "He is our friend."

"Yeah. A good friend. I miss him when he's not hanging around, but sometimes I'm not sure I did him any favor."

"What do you mean?"

"Maybe I should have told the Colonel. Maybe it would have been better to all be out in the open. They probably wouldn't have killed him. Hell, they didn't kill, Calley for Mai Lai. They'd have probably locked him up for a while, but by now he'd be out. By now it would all be over and not hanging over both our heads."

She hugged me tightly. "Don't beat yourself up, Sweetie. You did what you could. You did what you thought was right. You did the best you knew how. That's all and everything we ever do, and should be all that anyone asks."

After a while I said, "Thank you. I needed that."

"I know you did. This wasn't easy for you."

"It was necessary," I said. "I had to do this if I ever hoped to sleep with you again."

She smiled. "Soon, I hope."

We cuddled for quite a while, but it was getting very late.

Lily sat up in bed and said, "I know you're going to send me home so Toshi doesn't think Granny slept over, but I'd like to get a couple of things straight."

I sat up too. "Go ahead. Shoot."

"Tuco's never told you his side of this story, but you think he told Glowery's victim, this Newton character."

"Sure. They were trading war stories to decide whose was worst. What could be worse than Tuco's confession that he did a murder?"

"You know he probably thought he had to." Lily said.

"You never have to. You make a judgment and a choice. He was wrong. He'd told Newton this terrible thing, but Newton went to work for Glowery.

"Ghost could never know. If he knew, he owned Tuco. If Ghost owned Tuco, he owned me. He told me as much when we talked."

"And Tuco still didn't tell you? Didn't ask for your help?"

I shrugged. "Well he didn't. He threw dust in my eyes instead. Don't ask me why. I haven't got that part figured out.

"He cozies up to Newton on the island. Persuades Newton it's more noble to steal the truck than to take it to Mexico. They steal the truck. Tuco hides it. Ghost catches Newton again, but Newton can't tell him where Tuco hid the truck.

"But Newton didn't tell Glowery the secret?"

"Pure luck," I said. "Probably Ghost didn't know to ask. He then tells Tuco he's killed his friend. We know that Tuco knew before the cops did. Glowery probably told him as part of a threat, but he leaves Tuco enough time to get his stuff and get out of town.

"Tuco's not coming home any time soon."

"Tuco killed an old woman." She said it slowly as if testing the words..

"Tuco killed a wounded, helpless old woman we were supposed to protect." I said.

"I don't believe it."

"I don't believe you've got a choice."

"I can choose not to believe he did it!"

"So you choose to believe I did?"

"I don't want it to be either one of you," she said.

I gathered her in my arms and held her tight. "I don't either," I said. "He's my friend. He's loyal to me in his fashion, and I am loyal to him.

"I am sorry, sweetheart. Maybe I shouldn't have shared the burden of this, but I don't know how I could not. I know it's an old war, but I can't get away from it. I have to watch for Tuco and watch out for him. That has always been a burden to you, to us, whether or not you knew it."

"If I know nothing else I know I love you," she said. "And I know neither of you could have done this.

"Isn't it nice to think so," I said.

CHAPTER 24

I slept in late, got back to the cottage in time for lunch, and made myself a B.L.T.

I got a clean glass from the dish rack and found the last Poleeko Gold in the refrigerator. Out in the garden where I sipped the beer, I kept looking around hoping for the orange cat.

I guess he didn't like beer as well as milk.

After a while I went back in the cottage and made myself another sandwich. I was out of beer, so I filled the glass with water and went back to the garden. The sun was high and the day was warm. I remained where I was when the sandwich was finished and tried to think.

Dead, Glowery wasn't after Tuco. If Tuco worried about the CID I thought I could talk him out of that. Was the news about Glowery's death enough to bring him home?

I still didn't think so. I don't think of myself as superstitious, but at the moment I felt that way. My Granddad used to say that news comes in threes; that's superstition, but I knew what he meant. Sometimes the pattern is incomplete. I felt sure I was missing something. I had too many questions left, but no good way to answer them.

The sun felt very pleasant, a wonderful celebration of spring and a hint of the summer to come. I decided to stay in it.

I had dumped my files next to the couch when I started to plan the trap for Ghost. Floyd had a shredder in the garage. I borrowed an extension cord so I could put the shredder next to my garden chair. I hauled out my box of files sorting out cases and pages within cases. I made little piles of paper and stopped sorting once in a while to shred them.

There was a gentle breeze from the bay. There's a warm day weather pattern that I am very used to. If the sun warms the Central Valley enough, the rising air sucks the cooler ocean air in through the Golden Gate and into the valley across the Delta. The breeze was pleasant this afternoon, but sometimes it lifted one of my pages a foot or so from its pile. I got up to retrieve one when it was suddenly pounced upon by a loudly purring orange cat.

At least one of my friends was back. This time the cat would allow himself to be picked up and decided he could remain in a lap. We sat there for quite a while, petting, purring, and admiring each other.

I thought of the other paper I had not yet pounced on.

I shredded the pile I had already pulled and closed the box. The file labeled "Newton" in felt tipped pen was still by the couch. I left the box and took the file back to the garden where my friend and I sat while I examined the paperwork.

Here were my long notes from my conversation with Tuco about Newton. Here was the original signed contract from Theresa Garcia, now worth nothing since Tuco would never bill her for it. Here was a copy of my email sending her the modified contract. Here was her email address with the facsimile of her signature.

Then I noticed her email address: Yearning66.

The hair on my forearms stood up. Theresa Garcia had written the passionate note I had found in Tuco's email.

I grabbed my "Tuco" file and found the printout of her email to Tuco, and reviewed the contents again. "This is madness," she wrote. "You say you love me, but you won't tell me where you're going." Maybe she didn't know where he was, but she was a part of his life; she might well know his reasons.

Tuco's reasons were my biggest mystery. He's not the kind of guy who hides from trouble. If it was too much for him, he knew he could ask for help, and until now, often if not always, he would ask me.

"Fred," I said out loud, "Come back. I need a cat in my lap."

Fred and I sunned ourselves in the garden while I thought about what kind of approach I would make to Teri Garcia, an ambush interview, an email?

Not all decisions are rational.

I decided to ask for another personal interview. I decided on the direct approach, or maybe the garden, the cat, and the sun decided. I was tired of being George Duvall, ace detective full of tricky moves. I wanted peace and quiet, in my inner life as much as it was for the moment without.

I didn't call Garcia until a little after five o'clock. I simply told her I wanted to see her again and asked what hour would be convenient. She had a cancellation at 11 the next day. If an hour was enough she could fit me in.

I had breakfast with Floyd before I left.

"Sounds as if you've just about got this thing wrapped up," he said.

"If I can find out where he is," I said.

"Still got no clue?

"None," I said. "It's like he fell off the map."

I took a different route to Petaluma, across the Richmond/San Rafael Bridge, then north on 101.

She said, "Good Morning," at the door, "I'm having coffee if you would like some."

"I would," I said.

"Have a seat," she said and rolled away.

The house was very quiet but for the faint clatter of her coffee preparations. The only other sound was the pendulum of a grandfather clock. There was a faint scent of lemon in the air, perhaps from soap or wax.

Garcia returned with a complete coffee service on a wooden inlaid tray. I helped her put it on the small table between our chairs.

"I want to start with an apology," I said when we were settled. "I read a note you sent to Tuco in email. I didn't know it was you then. He's never seen it because I downloaded it from the mail server. I didn't recognize the email address until I read it on a print of your email to me yesterday afternoon.

"I read your note because I was looking for information. Perhaps that wasn't very ethical, but I didn't have to break in or do anything illegal to see it. I just opened email on his computer at my house. It's clear you are in love with him, and for some reason when we spoke you chose not to tell me. It's my guess you had to work at it pretty hard."

She blushed and looked down where she held her coffee cup and saucer.

"He told me I should tell no one," she finally said. "He said it would be dangerous for me if Glowery found out, and somebody else was coming who also might be dangerous. He thought I would be safe if no one knew."

"Hardly seems like much protection," I said. "Glowery had no conscience, and he had a lot of greed. If he knew he would have crushed you until you talked, and whether you talked or not he would have kept on crushing."

"If anybody scared me badly, I was supposed to tell them about the storage yard, a key taped to the bottom of his desk drawer, and C237."

"Putting my family at risk?"

"He was pretty sure it wouldn't happen. He was pretty sure Glowery would go after you first. Glowery knew about the two of you, he said. You would get to Glowery, and I would be more or less safe."

"We're lucky it worked out. I don't think I'm that good; I'm far short of a sure thing."

"He said you were tough and persistent. He said you knew Glowery about as well as anyone could. He said he had to hope that would be enough."

"And if he was here now he'd say thanks, Blondie, good job."

She allowed herself a smile of pleasure. "Yes he would."

"Did he say who else was coming?"

"Besides Glowery or his thugs?"

"That's what I'm asking," I said.

"Some sort of investigation. He didn't know exactly who, but he said there was a rumor so strong he couldn't ignore it. Somebody wanted to know about something that happened in Vietnam. It's about the death of a woman."

"Did he say who killed her?"

"He said it didn't really matter because it happened in the war. He said that you and he were the likely suspects. He said you'd be okay because you're good at keeping secrets and besides you used to be the Chief of Police. They would believe you. Nobody was going to believe him. If he denied it, they would think he was lying. He said he thought it was best for everybody if he went into hiding."

I was on the brink of asking her if she thought Tuco had killed the old woman. I decided not to ask. If she knew enough she could realize that if one of us had to be guilty, I must be the killer if he was innocent - not a thought I wanted in her head.

"It turns out this investigation probably isn't very dangerous," I said. I told her all about my conversation with Elrond.

"He didn't think the investigation could prove anything," she said. "He was afraid of what might happen if one of you thought he was cornered. Somebody might get hurt, he said."

That was true enough for any of us.

"I know he didn't tell you where he was going," I said. "Did he tell you anything about the place?"

"He called it out in the woods. He said there was no telephone, no cell service, and no Internet. He said he would be in town from time to time and he figured he might be able to read his email in the library. He'd have to travel further than town to get to cell service, but he would try to call when he could."

"Hmm. He can't be too far out. He expects to charge that phone. There must be electricity. Could be on a generator though," I said. After a while I said, "How are you doing without him?"

"I miss him terribly." Her eyes filled with tears. "I lost my legs when I was still very young. I never thought I could be with anyone. Over the years there have been offers but too many of them were like Newton, more about need or pity instead of love. I only got through it all because my Dad believed in me and taught me to be strong."

"You wouldn't get pity from Tuco."

She smiled. "I got love. I accused him of pity once before I knew him well. He just smiled and took off his shirt, unbuttoned his pants and showed me his colostomy. Wanted to show me that he had scars too, he said.

"Find him," she said. "Bring him back to me."

"Email him," I said. "Tell him we can brazen it out with the CID. Tell him we miss him. Tell him he can come home. I'll email him too."

"If he won't you've got to find him."

I said, "There are lots of woods out there. I'll do my best.".

CHAPTER 25

I had a burger for lunch at a drive in and drove back around the bay on the Lakeville Highway.

Fred wasn't in the garden. I went back to shredding files. My mind was more or less empty of everything but unanswered questions about Tuco. Maybe I was suffering from a failure of imagination; maybe I was just spent. I could email him too.

I wrote:

Hi Tuco,

I met your lady today for the second time, and this time I knew you were an item.

She's beautiful brother. She's brave, strong, worthy of my comrade. I think you can come home to her.

There's an investigation on about January1971, but don't worry about it. Maybe it's nothing but an Army whitewash. He's got everybody's name and address. We'll know soon enough if anything comes of it.

I don't know where you are or why you think you need to be there, but I can tell you it's more or less safe at home. Ghost's dead. The investigation might be a fake and if it isn't maybe the El Tee's warnings have made it pretty toothless. If we have to we can try to blame the old woman's death on Ghost. Hodiak may be out to get me, but he hasn't been seen or heard from yet.

Come home please. Or at least tell me how I can help.
Blondie.

I didn't send it off right away. I knew I was downplaying the CID too much. I sent it off sitting in the garden. After a while I was very glad to see Fred among the tulips. He trotted over smartly and settled in my lap. I tried to be present. I tried to focus on the purring cat head butting my palm, on the sun warming my face, and the lovely spring day in the garden.

I was not succeeding. My mind was many miles and years away. I could smell shit drenched in burning diesel on the firebase. I remembered the unending monsoon rain nearly warm as the present sun. I remembered fear, heat, anger, effort, and exhaustion. I remembered how I struggled to keep my honor, how I fought to find my courage and to live it. I remembered being angry. I was angry again.

Perhaps Fred felt it. He rolled under my hand on to his back, attacked my arm with his claws and bit me gently, still purring.

"I'm not mad at you, Fred." I said aloud. If he could have talked he would have said, "I'm a cat in your lap. Pay attention," and now I could. We sat for perhaps an hour when my phone rang.

"I'm back at the house," Lily said. "Why don't you come over for dinner?"

I decided to shave again. I showered and changed too. Fred's company had been welcome, but he left orange fur all over my pants.

Lily had been thinking about our dinner long before she called me. She served fried chicken and hot German potato salad. I know her cooking and I know the chicken had been soaked in buttermilk much earlier in the day. We ate an early dinner on the patio, looking out over the canyon, tall glasses of ice water, a Poleeko Gold for me, and white wine for her.

I cleared away the dishes and loaded the dishwasher.

Dusk began now. We sat at the patio table in the fading light holding hands. We'd been chatting away through dinner, but now fell quiet in the growing darkness.

Finally she said, "I've thought a lot about what you told me the other night."

"About Tuco?"

"And about you too."

"Well you knew most of it before."

"I knew he got wounded, and you thought it was your fault. I didn't know he'd killed someone. I didn't know you are afraid he might despair."

"Does it show?"

"Always has. I just didn't know," she said. "You're very patient with him, even if he makes you mad, and you're respectful of what he thinks or feels, even when you don't agree. And you bend the rules for him."

"Isn't that how you treat a friend?"

"Yes, but often you have more in common with other friends than you have with Tuco. And you give him more room than most. Sometimes he walks all over you, but you never flinch."

"I'm just vigilant."

"It's not just him. You look out for people."

"Ma'am," I said in my best John Wayne impression, "that's what a peace maker is supposed to-do."

"Maybe too much," she said. "People don't always want to be looked out for."

"Sometimes somebody has to."

"The other night you talked about sleeping with me again. Regularly, I assume.

"Uh-huh."

"I want you to know. I want you back, but if you don't want to yet, you don't have to. I know you love me. I know you will always love me. We're apart right now, but it's not for lack of love. You'll be back."

I squeezed her hand. "Thank you," I said. "I think I need you more now than I ever did, but I can't come back inside yet. I don't know where I'm going or why. I don't know how to get there."

She smiled and put her hand gently over my mouth. "Sometimes the only way out is through. There's something you have to do."

"Yeah," I said, but I didn't know how to do it.

We held each a long time in the moonlight before we went in to bed.

When I went home to the cottage that night, I checked my email. Nothing yet.

In the morning, I finished up my shredding. Fred was nowhere to be found. I boxed up the files I meant to keep and drove back to the storage yard. They were open for business. The crime scene tape was gone. You could only see the evidence of the gunfight if you were looking for it pretty hard. I noticed new paint patches that I guessed were meant to protect the steel exposed by lead. The most visible signs were some marks on the ground where the van and the man had died.

At my container, I returned my files to their bottom drawer. Looking at my boat, I remembered the last time I had it out. Tuco and I had gone camping, fished for trout at Miller Lake in Oregon. I knew I'd like to do that again.

I stopped for lunch on the Richmond parkway where I could treat myself to an A&W root beer float. When I got home I made phone calls.

Hodiak's name was being circulated as a person of interest. Something must have turned up in a search, but no one would tell me what they'd found. There was no sign of Hodiak in Solano, Contra Costa, San Joaquin, or Alameda County.

Schooner was my source in Contra Costa County, and we talked about it.

"I don't think he'll bother your daughter in Fremont," he said. "Hodiak might not even know she's there."

"I know his crew picked me up once in Fremont. I've got to assume they followed me from there."

"Fine, I'd still think El Sobrante would be the primary target. You and Glowery both lived there too long nose to nose."

"He knows about El Cerrito too," I said.

"Yeah, but in El Cerrito he knows about Floyd. I don't think he would take Floyd too lightly after what happened to Horse."

"Who's Horse?"

"Street name for the guy Floyd capped."

"Bob, do you know anybody in Fremont?"

"Sure."

"Could you try to arrange for patrol to drive by Karen's house? I'll call Vinnie; I think he can make the same arrangement for Lily in El Sobrante. That's not perfect, but it will do until I can make better arrangements."

The group at the church was on my calendar for that afternoon. There was no reply to my email when I left for group.

They wanted to know all about it.

"Now I know what you were on about the other day," MACSOG said.

"You guys were right." I said. "I couldn't let the gangster have his way. Tough part is he was also one of us, or one of mine at least. He was in Recon with Tuco and me."

"How did you feel?" Al asked.

"I puked in a corner," I said.

"How about your pants?" HP asked.

"My pants were fine," I said. "That was never a problem I had."

"What about Tuco?" MACSOG asked.

"I don't know. I found out he still uses email. He left his computer behind because he's hiding where there is no Internet. His girl says he sometimes uses computers at the library. I wrote him a note, but haven't heard anything yet."

"He'll hear about Glowery."

"I hope so."

"Will he come home?"

I thought about Lily telling me that I always look out for people. People don't always want looking after. I thought about the CID. "Maybe that's up to him," I said. I was a little surprised how hard it was to say it.

Al raised an eyebrow. "Has something else happened, Duvall?"

CID happened, but I couldn't talk about that. I couldn't say the CID was dangerous. I couldn't tell these guys Tuco would not be found out. I couldn't talk about it.

Al was still looking at me.

"Nothing," I said. "Nothing," and that's pretty much what I said in the rest of group.

No email again when I checked.

I rang up Lily and said, "I'd like to barbecue a steak or two, unless you've got other plans."

"I love it when I don't have to cook," she said.

"I'd like to pack a bag," I said. "I can sleep out in Tuco's room. I wouldn't be dangerous to you there."

"I'm not afraid of you," Lily said.

"You should be," I said, "but maybe you should be more afraid of Hodiak."

"I've got a gun, mister, and I know how to use it."

"Two guns would be better," I said. "That's why I want to sleep over."

"You don't need to ask my permission, Duvall. You're an owner in this house."

"Yes, dear. Of course. I just didn't want to surprise you."

"Uh, huh. Just looking out for me again."

I let that pass with some difficulty. Much later snuggling in bed under a warm comforter she said, "It's okay with me if you fall asleep." Of course I didn't. Vigilance is a bitch.

When she was sound asleep, I extricated myself very carefully. I know where she keeps her Ladysmith so I had to be careful. There is an Army legend that troops aren't responsible for anything they do in the first ten seconds after being awakened from a sound sleep.

In Tuco's room I cranked up the space heater to get warm again. Our spring days can be quite warm, but the nights stay cool longer.

I checked my email again, and I didn't fall asleep for at least an hour.

I checked the email again when I got up. I shaved, showered, and dressed. At breakfast Lily tried to spoil me with eggs, biscuits, sausage gravy, orange juice, and hot coffee. I read everything in the West Contra Costa Times front to back. Glowery was no longer on the front page.

"Doing anything special today?" Lily asked as she poured my second cup of coffee.

I grinned. "I could use a job."

"There are several," she said. "You can take your choice: mowing, weeding, windows, and prepping the raised beds."

Weeding on our slope would be the hardest. We were trying to encourage ice plant to take over, but it hadn't yet. I got out the mower instead. The compost bin was full of ready stuff so I spread it among the raised beds where we grow some vegetables. After mowing I loaded the grass clippings in the composter, covered the top with a layer of old compost for a starter, and wet it down

I raked the old compost into the raised beds.

I make my own tomato cages from PVC pipe. They're disassembled and bagged at the end of the season. I found the bags in the garden shed and put them together again.

Lily knew several things she wanted to plant. Late in the afternoon, we drove over to Adachi Florist and Nursery to pick put some veggie starts.

I checked email before dinner, and I called Schooner. There was still no sign of Hodiak, but Bob was glad to know I was back at the house.

Lily cooked. We had a quiet evening at home watching a little T.V.

In the morning Lily and I planted together. I love gardening. The plants never talk back.

After lunch I got out the Windex and the step ladder. Lily and I always do windows together. I get the outside because I can reach the high ones with a step ladder. Lily does the inside. We do each window together, pointing out streaks we see left in the other's work. We do this every spring. When Karen was still home we did it in two teams, Karen paired with Tuco.

Lily surprised me when the job was done. She'd poured ice over a six pack of Poleeko Gold sometime around lunch. At the patio table looking out over our canyon, I felt momentarily at rest.

The El Tee called.

"The guys are going along," he said. "I expect CID to be buried in meaningless answers."

"Good," I said. "That's what they want. I wish I knew who was really doing the asking and why, but I'll settle for getting them off our back."

"So how's the hunt," he said. "Have you heard anything from Tuco yet?

"No."

"What are your next steps?"

"What do you mean, next steps," I said. Aren't you the guy who told me to leave him alone?"

"Yeah that was me. I just didn't think you could let it go after what you went through with Ghost."

"You'd be right," I said. "I still want to find him. I don't know why anymore, but I do."

"You want help? I could be there in half a day."

"Thanks El Tee. What would be the point? I don't know where to look, and I wouldn't have any use for you yet."

"Two minds may be better than one."

"We are already two minds. Are we better? I just need to wait. I need him to answer. Maybe I have always needed him to answer."

"Well I'm here if you need me."

Next day I tackled the weeding on our slope. I got an early start. I set the alarm for 5:30, showered, shaved, dressed, and checked the email by 6 o'clock. I had a bowl of corn flakes with banana and milk, and I started work in the cool of the morning about 6:30.

I had a rubber mat for my knees, and a trowel, and fork for digging weeds. I wore coveralls and wide straw hat. I brought along a supply of bags, and a bottle of water.

The slope is simply the side of a hill behind our house.

The raised beds where we planted the vegetables were built just behind the retaining wall. Behind the raised beds to the neighbor's fence we nurtured a small orchard. There were two cherry trees, one a Bing and the other a Rainier. There were two peach trees and an apricot. There was a Meyer lemon that always threatened to engorge its neighbors. There was an apple tree, but I'm not sure what kind. The apples are yellow powdered with red stripes. I know they taste pretty good.

There are lots of places on the slope that I can climb up to pretty easily, going from one tree to another grabbing branches and bracing myself against the fruit tree trunks. That won't let me all the way up, and it doesn't hold me very well.

I find its best to extend my ladder and brace its feet against the back of the raised beds. I can climb without any big struggle and I can weed without spending all my strength trying not to roll down the hill. I climb the ladder to the top, weed right, left, and through it. I take a couple of steps down and do it again. When I get to the bottom, I move the ladder again.

I worked steadily and well, knowing I would want it done before the afternoon heat. By lunch time there was only some little of it left. I washed my hands and while I was at it my forearms, face, and neck.

I checked the email before I went out to lunch.

He wrote:

Rogers Rangers.

Teri's the best. She's tough enough to take me as I am. Yes, I'm in love.

Best thing you can do for me is keep her safe.

Thanks for Ghost. I owed him for Newton.

There's another ambush out there somewhere that's not been sprung yet. I can smell it, and I'm staying put. Stay where you are and you'll be safe.

I am not paranoid. I just need to stay away.

I had another email from Teri Garcia. She edited the most personal parts out of his email, and forwarded me her version of his message which wasn't much different than what he'd said directly to me.

Lily and I ate lunch, bread and soup on the patio with the umbrella up. I drank a couple of glasses of iced water had another beer.

I had printed out the email for Lily.

"What will you do," she asked.

"Guess I'll finish weeding the slope."

After lunch I did. I cleaned the tools, put away the ladder, took another shower, and changed clothes.

I sat on the patio with the umbrella up for another hour. Then I called Al Starr and asked for an appointment.

CHAPTER 28

When I called, Al asked me how much time I'd need.

"I don't know," I said. "Depends on how much I bleed, I guess."

"Could you come to the house at eight?"

I set my alarm for six and left the house at seven with plenty of time. I put the top down on the car, and wore a wool jacket and a cap to keep my hair in order. I am sure it was a pretty drive, but I drove it on autopilot, thinking about what I meant to say, and what I hoped to gain.

I trusted Al. I trusted him at least as much as I trust anyone, but Lily. None the less, I knew he could be evasive and tricky if he thought he was doing it for me or for that matter for anyone else.

How could you ever be sure who he was doing it for? That was the problem. In group, Al's client was the group. A healthy group was good for all of us. If Al saw you alone, he was treating you, not the group. For most of the guys that was fine. So far as I could tell there was no one in the group who were friends outside. Tuco and I were unique, so what were Al's loyalties when he treated us?

What was best for me might not be best for Tuco. What was best for Tuco might not be best for me. What was best for Tuco and me as a pair of friends who wanted to preserve that friendship might be an entirely different matter. Al, I felt sure, was threading an ethical needle as a therapist. In fact I wasn't at all sure that it was ethical for him as a therapist to try to treat us both at once. Al wasn't just a therapist; he was a fellow vet and a minister in the Christian faith. Maybe as a vet and minister he was beyond the rules.

I didn't share Al's problem. I was in this for myself. Tuco? I was no longer so sure I was in it for Tuco.

Why should I care about Tuco? He had locked me out of the Newton case. He manipulated me. He had more regard for Lily than for me. He had left me stranded with the problem of Ghost and the weapons. He had committed theft, though a well meaning one, and he had left me holding the bag. He had run away to hide and told his girlfriend to lie about it if she could.

What was I doing this for? What did I want Al to do for me? Two things maybe. If I could manipulate him into telling me where Tuco was, I would.

He knew Tuco and I were not too open about what had happened to us in Vietnam. We hadn't told him everything yet. At least I hadn't. He knew we protected each other, like an old married couple he said. Maybe if I told him the final truth, maybe if I told him about the old woman's murder, he could tell me where Tuco was - if in fact he knew.

On the other hand, maybe I didn't much care what he told me. Maybe I just needed to be free of obsession. Tuco and I were tangled with each other like a couple of tar babies. At the moment I was pretty sick of that. Maybe I just wanted out.

I had the usual trouble finding parking on old Martinez's narrow streets. Al was out on the big front porch of his craftsman house with a mug of coffee.

"Want some?" he asked. "We've got both kinds. She drinks full strength, and I drink decaf."

"I could use the real deal with a little milk," I said.

Al got me coffee, and led me back to his home office, a converted bedroom. In the old days no one thought a bedroom needed too much space.

We sat in remarkably comfortable wooden chairs. His doubled as his desk chair; it was on wheels and had a swivel base. He sat with his back to his desk which looked out over a small yard. I had the same model of seat, but with no moving parts. There was a small coffee table between us where we could put down our mugs on any of a fair collection of different coasters. I selected one, put down my mug, and waited.

He didn't start with therapy, at least not directly.

"How's the hunt for Tuco?" he asked.

He'd heard my updates to the group so there wasn't really anything new to tell except about Tuco's email.

"Another ambush not yet sprung," Al said. "Hmm. How do you feel about that?"

Therapy had begun. "Frustrated," I said. "I seem to have done everything I know how to do for him but he hasn't come home yet. Maybe he doesn't want to. Maybe he doesn't care to show himself. I suppose in the end you can only know somebody else through what he is willing to show you, and right now Tuco's showing me nothing at all."

"How do you feel about this new girlfriend?"

"She's strong. She'll expect him to be who he is, and she can accept what happened to him. There's lots who can't, but you know that. It's not just Vietnam. There are many women for whom the colostomy is too much. She's a double amputee. She knows better than most that we've all got scars."

"Good to hear," Al said, "but that's not quite what I asked. Let me put that another way. Are you jealous?"

I laughed. "No, no. Lily's more than enough for me! Why should I be jealous?"

Al laughed too. "Well, I have said you are like an old married couple. I never thought there was anything sexual in it, but you have a bond that has lasted for many years. He has lived in your house for most of them. You've survived together, not just in Vietnam, but in other adventures since. If Tuco is serious about this woman, he may be moving away from your family and he might not be coming back."

"Tuco will always be family," I said, "no matter how far away he is or whether he chooses to come back. Teri would be good for him. She's much younger. Maybe still young enough for children. It would mean he was finally getting on with his life."

"Would that be good for you?"

"What do you mean?"

"Would you be getting on with your life too? Or would you be calling, hanging around, and still trying to watch out for Tuco?"

"I'd still care about him," I said, "but I would try to keep out of his way and let him have his own life."

"Try? What is this try? Give him a friendly divorce, Duvall. Give him his rest, Duvall. Let him find his own peace."

I was shocked how quickly and easily I wept. "I don't think I can trust him to find it by himself."

"No one else can do it," Al said. "If you are always there, I don't think he stands a chance.

"You two are deeply entwined with each other, tied up in a knot I can't quite see yet. I know that you feel guilty because you were walking point the day you got 'bushed and Tuco got hurt, but that's no reason you can't let him go where he has a good chance of his own happiness."

Still dripping tears from my chin, I said, "I just want him to come home. I miss him."

"You just want to know he is still your friend," Al said. "That's your guilt talking. He's been avoiding you, and you're afraid that means he hasn't forgiven you even yet.

"You weren't the damned VC Duvall. You didn't set off that charge. You weren't squeezing the clacker on that mine! You didn't do it. Charley did. You didn't make Tuco go to Vietnam. Sam did; the country did. There's nothing to forgive."

"Yes there is."

"Tell me."

I decided to tell him. Despite my pain, I knew this was my chance. Tuco did solo sessions with Al too. Al might still know where he was. If Al knew anything at all about where Tuco was, I might persuade him that Tuco was a danger to himself or others, and Al might give him up. Tuco with his present fear and past sins was a sure danger to himself if not to others.

"It's a long story," I said. "Maybe I didn't mean to be Tuco's friend, but he got assigned to Recon as some kind of punishment. He didn't have infantry training. I took him on as my RTO and taught him the ropes. After a while he didn't mind the radio so much and didn't want to leave. He used to say that when he got home he'd buy his own radio so he could piss on it on his back porch."

"And the point is?" Al asked.

"He's a little weird about authority and rules. He did do what he was told. He did do what he had to do, but often he resented doing it. Me too, I guess."

"Sure. That's normal."

"Division intel put us on a road expecting NVA. I thought they were crazy at the time. We hadn't seen NVA for months. It was as if they went to sleep. My lieutenant told me to put out an Alpha Alpha on our back trail."

"What's an Alpha Alpha?"

"What we called a claymore booby trap.

"Anyway this old lady walked up on Tuco and me when we were putting it out. She was wounded. We took her into the platoon, but it was too late in the day to get her on a chopper and get her out. We made her a place to sleep. She was pretty noisy. The El Tee was a little strange about it, probably because he couldn't order it done. He said he thought we should shoot her if the NVA showed up because her noise would give away our position."

"And what's this got to do with you and Tuco?"

"The Alpha Alpha went off at three in the morning. We had movement on the opposite side of our night defensive position. Guys were shooting at movement. Guys were blowing off claymores. I..."

could not say it. I could not be the one that told Al that Tuco was a killer. It should be between them. I should not be involved.

"Go on," Al said. "What happened?"

I had to say something. I was in too deep. Someone said, "I killed her. I got scared she might give us away so I shot her," and it was me.

It was a terrible lie. I'm not good at lying but hoped to get away with it, and I was scared I might, scared of what it might mean for me with Al, with the group, with the world for that matter with anybody else in my life.

I felt sweat clinging to my hair line. A trickle of it rolled off my nose. My skin felt cold and clammy; I was light headed; I puked in the waste basket at Al's feet.

Al put his hand on my shoulder until the spasms stopped and I could breathe again.

"Are you okay?" he asked.

I nodded.

"I've got medicine for this," he said. "Let me get some with a glass of water."

I felt clear headed and disoriented all at once. The details of the room were suddenly starkly clear, but as if I had never seen them before.

There were red textured curtains on Al's window over the yard, and a red covered valance. The ceiling and top half of the room was papered with an old style of wall paper, a pattern of tiny roses on stems repeated over and over again. There was wainscoting on the wall and a wood panel below that. The paneling looked pretty good, but somehow out of alignment, as if settling and shifting in this old house distorted them, or maybe Al had done the paneling and not quite got it right. There was a strange pattern of scratches on the paneling next to the window. I found myself thinking that maybe the floors tilted slightly away from me toward Al's desk.

"Here. Take these," Al said. He handed me a couple of pills and a tall, red, aluminum cup.

I swallowed the pills and drank all of the water.

"That's quite a revelation," Al said. "One I didn't expect. I had some suspicions and I have prayed about them, but what you said makes me think I've got it all wrong."

"It's true," I lied. "It wasn't easy to say. Most of the time it's not something I want to admit even to myself." It seemed easy to continue the lie. "I'm ashamed of what I did.

What makes it worst of all was that I was always the guy who wanted to be sure he was shooting at the enemy and not somebody else. I didn't want to fire my weapon unless I heard them firing theirs or saw their weapons first."

"And what's this got to do with Tuco?"

"It's what we agreed about," I said. "We, Tuco and me, were always at pains to keep from shooting civilians. He kind of idolized me about that. I don't think he knows for sure I shot her, but he thinks no one else could have done it. A little while ago I learned there was an investigation about all of this. I told you he's funny about authority. I think he's afraid if the right guy asks the questions he won't be able to help telling the guy about me."

I easily lied about Tuco. I simply put my thoughts in his head and turned them around. In the lie he thought about me as I thought about him. If there was a lie it was simply that I knew Tuco wouldn't really talk about me anymore than I would talk about him. I couldn't do it. I wouldn't do it. Maybe I could only talk to Lily about it because I knew she would deny the truth of it.

"There's more," I said. "There's more that makes it worse. There was no enemy. The movement we had was only a herd of pigs. We killed more than a dozen of them. We had a barbecue."

Al closed his eyes, leaned his head forward and pinched the bridge of his nose. He kept his mouth closed, but his lips moved in and out sometimes. He sat there silently for far more than a minute. He opened his eyes and started looking around the room. He looked at the ceiling. He looked at the walls left and right. He would not look at me.

"Would it surprise you if I told you Tuco told me something else? Would it surprise you if I told you that Tuco said he killed the old woman? Can you think why he might do that?"

Of course I could. It was easy. All I had to do was put my motivations in Tuco's mouth.

"He probably did it to protect me," I said. "He would probably rather take the blame than tell someone else the truth." I knew he'd been telling the truth, but as far as Al was concerned, I wanted him to see it the other way.

218

"True enough," said Al. "True enough for one of you at least. Do you know what a sin eater is, Duvall?"

"No."

"In the old days, people would bring food as gifts for someone dead or departed. Some shunned member of the community would eat the food, and in old folklore that meant the sin eater ate and absorbed the sins of the dead, letting him get into heaven.

"That's what's happening here, Duvall. One of you is lying. One of you at least is a sin eater for the other and maybe both. I don't know how to get either of you out of your fix without the truth."

"I'm telling the truth," I said.

"You are as best you can," Al said. "I'm just not at all sure that's good enough. Give me a second Duvall. I've got something here that might help us out of this fix."

He swiveled in his chair and faced the desk and window. He opened the bottom right hand drawer which proved to be a file drawer. I could see the hanging pendaflex folders and tabs. Rummaging through this he brought out a page of paper, glanced at it, hesitated, and pushed it across the coffee table to me.

I picked it up. I was looking at a sketch map, probably drawn with a black marker, labeled by hand, and photocopied, perhaps several times. It was a sketch of an exit from I-5. A road labeled Hatchery Lane led west and met another road called W.A. Barr Lane. After some meandering, Barr Lane led around the edge of something called Lake Siskiyou and there was another turn marked onto a road called Castle Lake. This whole course was darker than the rest and there were arrows along the route to direct you.

"I don't do this lightly," Al said. "I've prayed about this quite a bit, ever since Tuco told me his story. I didn't want to believe it. I still don't, neither yours nor his, but maybe there's only one way to the truth. You've got to have it out between you. Soldiering isn't widely understood to be an altruistic act, but..."

"What do you mean 'altruistic'?" I asked.

"I mean you didn't do it for yourselves. You did it for each other. You did it because you thought you ought to, because your country asked you to do it. You didn't want to. You, Duvall, didn't believe in the war, but you went anyway. You did it because your country asked, and you thought it had a right to, because you were a citizen, a part of the community,

"You did it for honor. You did it because you thought you owed it to yourselves. And you never meant to harm any who did not mean harm to you."

"That's true," I said, "but it's no different than a lot of the damned - if- you -do, damned - if - you- don't choices that people make every day."

"I don't believe in damned choices," Al said. "I always believe there is a third way.

"Not always," I said. "So where is this?" I asked, shaking his map at him.

"Mt. Shasta," Al said. "We've got a church camp up Castle Lake road on the right. You can't miss it. There's a sign. When Tuco said he needed to hide out for a while, I got him on up there as a caretaker. I didn't lie, Duvall. I told you he didn't tell me where he was hiding. He didn't. I told him where to hide."

"I pray to God this is the right choice. Don't shame me, Duvall. Find the third way." He told me some more about the camp.

We stood together. I embraced him. As I left I thought there were tears in his eyes too.

I called Lily as soon as I was back on the road.

"Al told me where he is," I said. "Al's known all along. Tuco's way up north near Mt. Shasta at a church camp. He's out of cell range and off the grid. The only electricity he's got is from a generator. They heat and refrigerate with propane. There's no phone. I've got to get up there. I'm coming home to pack. Could you make me something for the road, please? And maybe a thermos of coffee. I'll take off right after lunch."

"Slow down, dear. I'm so glad. I'll make sandwiches, and then you can go bring him home."

Somebody else had been carrying the load too. I was still in the car, but I rang up the El Tee.

"Bookman." he growled.

"El Tee. It's Blondie. I've found him. I know where he is. I'm headed that way after lunch."

"Is that smart, Blondie? He's pretty paranoid. Do you really want to do this? Are you sure you don't want some help? I could catch a red eye."

"Nah," I said. "You can't get a direct flight there or even close. Closest minor airport is maybe a hundred miles away. This is really a one man job. If he's nervous he'll be more nervous with two of us. You stay there in Milwaukee and I'll let you know how it comes out."

"Where'd you find him?"

"Well find isn't quite the right word. He's at a church camp outside the little town of Mt. Shasta. I'll be driving up that way after lunch. There's a lake high in the mountains nearby. It's called Castle Lake. It's named after some rock formations near there called Castle Crags. The camp is somewhere on the road to the lake. My shrink told me about it. My shrink helped him hide there."

"Well let me know if there's anything at all I can do."

"Thanks, El Tee. I'll be in touch."

I didn't pack much, just an overnight bag. I wasn't going to stay long if Tuco wouldn't come down. It was my job to tell him he was safe and he could come home. Al might think I was the killer, but Al was never going to blab about that. Even if Tuco wasn't convinced, at least I would have planted the seed, and I could visit him again until he was ready to come out of the woods.

Lily had made French onion soup for lunch with floating crusts of bread and cheese. For a lunch at our house it was quite elaborate. I briefly thought she went all out to give me a send off meal.

A fresh pot of coffee brewed while we were eating lunch. She told me she'd made roast beef sandwiches for the trip. She put the rest of the coffee in a thermos.

She didn't tell me the rest of her plan until I took my overnight bag to the car and she brought hers too.

"What's this?" I asked.

"I'm coming. You might need me."

"This isn't a walk in the park," I said. "Tuco's my friend, but some would call him a fugitive killer. He might not just wave and invite us in. I'd rather you stayed here."

"And I'd rather not. You think I can stay home and wait? We know there's no cell service where he is. What am I supposed to do if I don't hear from you in the next day or two."

I grinned. "I'd usually say call the cops."

"Don't be an idiot. Just let me ride along. I'll stay out of your way. We can work that out when we get there."

I knew I couldn't win an argument with her. "Get in," I said.

I decided to drive the speed limit. I-5 is flat and straight north of Sacramento. I could probably have eaten up the drive in four or five hours, but there would be no point. I wanted to approach Tuco in the morning. There are too many shadows at night, in the mind as well as the light. In the morning we would both be fresh and alert and I would be rested if I drove the distance quietly and took a room for the night.

I didn't drink the coffee. I was so jacked up about finding Tuco that I was afraid with coffee there'd be little chance I'd fall asleep when I found a bed. I told Lily she'd be better off if she could fall asleep.

Though there's a fair amount of truck traffic on any weekday, it wasn't too bad. The road goes north through rural California. Sometimes I would drive up on a knot of cars, but nothing so snarled as the freeways near San Francisco Bay or worse, Southern California.

Traveling this way one often sees the same cars over distance and time. There are legal limits. You end up traveling with everyone else who obeys those limits.

At least that's what I told myself when I kept seeing the same black Mustang in my rear view mirror. It was probably only coincidence, and not Hodiak, though it seemed far less of a coincidence after we stopped in the late afternoon to eat our picnic.

We dawdled at the rest stop for a good hour to eat our sandwiches and stretch our legs. After the rest we hit the road again and I was startled to see the black Ford in my rear view mirror again, but maybe he had stopped somewhere for a bite too.

Better to err on the side of caution. I asked Lily to get the binoculars out of the glove box take a look if she got a chance. She'd never met Hodiak, but I thought her description might be clear enough. Unfortunately he lagged behind other vehicles and she couldn't get a good look.

The road north of Redding changes dramatically. It rises gradually through some hills and crosses Shasta Lake, a big reservoir from a dam on the Sacramento River.

The town of Mt. Shasta is hard by the mountain of that name, tall, majestic, and snow covered that spring; it looked like the Paramount pictures logo, impossible to ignore. We booked a room in town.

Lily suggested a couple of stiff drinks at the bar before we retired for the night.

"You need to get to sleep," she said. "Tomorrow is also just another day."

Sleep came more easily than I expected. I was probably snoring within minutes of crawling into bed.

CHAPTER 29

We checked out of the motel and ate breakfast at a busy coffee shop. The locals wore work boots, jeans, denim shirts, and ball caps. From time to time someone would join the crowd in dress shoes, pleated trousers, white shirt, tie, and sport coat. The ball cap guys greeted those wearing ties as one of their own.

I suppose we might fit in as senior citizen tourists though I broke that dress code a little with the formality of a sports coat over my tee shirt, jeans and trainers. I couldn't take off the jacket as others did with a gun under my arm.

We ate in a booth. I had link sausage, eggs, and hash brown potatoes with good black coffee. Lily had pancakes with strawberry jam. We smiled and nodded at every curious glance. I took a second cup of coffee and asked for a large glass of orange juice before we left.

W.A. Barr road led to a surprisingly upscale neighborhood surrounding a small lake behind a dam across the narrow neck of a box canyon. Developers here built contemporary, spacious homes much newer than developments around the older Shasta Lake.

I drove all around the lake, past Castle Lake road, to make sure of the layout. The road ended at a marina with a campground. I could see a few fishing boats going out. I turned around and went back and drove up Castle Lake road.

The road was paved at first, fairly steep, and finally no longer paved. There was a chain gate across the entrance driveway at the church camp. A long drive passed some boulders and a field of manzanita before rising through the trees to a fair sized log building with large shutters fastened open to the view of snow capped Mt. Shasta.

I kept driving. I didn't want to make too quick an approach to Tuco until I had a good idea of the whole layout. I was beginning to suspect I was in a bit of a box. W.A. Barr Lane looked to be the one way in and maybe the one way out. As promised Castle Lake road led past the barricaded driveway for the church camp to Castle Lake and ended in a small parking lot with campsites and a gravel boat ramp.

We paused there for several minutes enjoying the view of Castle Lake while I figured things out.

"Here's our tactical situation," I said. "We're in a long cul de sac and we're approaching someone who may be off balance. Yes, Tuco's our friend but we know he's apparently paranoid and fearful. We'll take the car down the hill and park it, obscurely if we can, on the other side of the Church camp."

I pulled out my cell phone to verify our theory.

"Look no bars," I said. Cell phones won't work. I want you to stay with the car at first. I'll walk into the camp very openly. Maybe I'll whistle. I don't want Tuco to think I'm sneaking up on him. If everything goes well, I'll come back down. Tuco should be able to open the gate and we can drive in.

"I expect to be able to walk back here in maybe thirty minutes. If you don't see me by then, drive back to Mt. Shasta and get the cops. If you hear gunfire, put the car in gear and get out of here quick.

"Is that clear.?"

"You think he'd shoot you?" She asked.

"Not really, but we have to plan for it. You read my email. He's hiding and bunkered up expecting something tricky. I don't really know how scared he is or of what, but he might shoot first and ask questions later. He might shoot before realizes that it's me.

"Do you know what to do?"

"You said you want me to stay in the car and take off if I hear gunshots or you don't come back?"

I had expected an argument but she made none.

"Yes. Good," I said. "One more thing. If he's really paranoid he may work out a way to watch the road, and maybe not just the entrance to the driveway. He's not likely to be on your side of the road, but you never know. I'll drive down real slow. I know you're not used to this, but look for anything that looks as if it doesn't belong there, a metallic flash, the leaves of bushes or trees drier than those around them, footprints or tracks in the dirt that suggest someone left the road."

"Okay," she said.

I drove down very slowly. We saw nothing on the road or in the trees and brush. If there was anybody hiding there, he was very good, but of course Tuco had been with Recon and was very good.

We passed the driveway and I found a wide spot in the road to park about four hundred yards on. I took the car out of gear, put the parking brake on and left the motor running.

We both got out to trade seats. We kissed each other before she slid in behind the wheel.

"Don't worry, sweetie. Remember he's our friend. I don't think he'll forget that."

I tried to follow my program as exactly as I could. I stepped over the chain and walked straight up the middle of the road whistling, not so much to show I hadn't a care in the world, but rather to warn Tuco I was on my way carefree, and maybe he ought to have a look.

The driveway threaded between large boulders and trees, mostly sugar pines, toward the long building, maybe a community hall or a kitchen and dining room big enough for a small church. There were windows but without glass. Hinged from the top of each window was a sheet of plywood that could cover the window. The windows were open and the plywood sheets propped to shade the openings with a wooden brace.

I caught glimpses through a patch of brushy woods of what seemed to be an old trailer a bit behind the building and a couple of hundred feet to the north. I could hear a stream some way off to my right.

Dirt erupted five or six feet in front of me as I heard the crack of a rifle shot. I dived and rolled for cover behind a large boulder. My pistol was already in my hand and I couldn't remember pulling it from the holster under my shoulder.

Combat reflexes are wonderful but dangerous because they happen without thought. I'd have to watch myself I shouldn't have to do any shooting. Lily should be tearing down the road to get the cops. What I really needed to do was stay loose, stay alive, escape, evade, and stall.

I was pretty sure the rifle was fired from the general direction of the big building, though I had seen nothing.

Was he still there or was he moving, trying to close in. I slowed my breathing by taking deeper breaths and for several minutes I tried to listen for any hint of movement.

Instead I got another rifle shot whining in the wind as it ricocheted off my boulder.

He hadn't moved. At least I didn't think he had. The shot was his way of telling me he knew where I was, maybe thinking to flush me out or drive me back.

I had worked out a possible escape route. There was a stand of manzanita behind me. If his elevation wasn't great there was a good chance I could get into it without leaving the cover of the boulder. The manzanita wouldn't stop a bullet as well as the rock, but he'd be a whole lot less sure of where I was.

I stayed on my belly and tried to low crawl backwards under the brush.

A bullet clipped a small rock near the heel of my left foot.

I scrambled back to the shelter of the boulder.

I could see the far end of the building. He seemed to be shooting from somewhere up there. Even if I didn't hit him, the .45 slug from my Kimber would make a hell of a racket and remind him I was armed, so I took the shot and rattled the sideboards of the hall.

And I listened again. I could hear grasshoppers whirring about. There was a cricket. Further away a hawk screamed.

Maybe I could make it to the manzanita with a slightly steeper angle.

"Don't try it, Duvall," Tuco said quietly.

I couldn't see him. He was in the manzanita off the right of my boulder. He was Recon trained and just as good as ever. I never heard cracked twig, a gravel scrape, nor a thump of footstep.

I had waited too long

"If you get in that brush we'd be even up. Your short gun might be better than my rifle. Leave the pistol on the ground and back away. Go away. I won't shoot you if you leave."

My heartbeat was a thunder my ears and I was suddenly drenched in sweat.

"How do I know that, Tuco."

"Maybe you don't, but I haven't shot you yet, but I will if I have to.

"And what about me," Lily called. "Are you going to shoot me Tuco? Kill George, and I think you have to."

I think we both turned toward her voice with some confusion. She was walking up the drive at a steady pace with no cover whatever.

"Lily," I screamed. "Go away. I told you to stay in the car."

"Yes you told me, George, but I didn't and don't agree.

She smiled ruefully and kept on walking. "No need for me to leave, George. He won't shoot me. He would never shoot me. I don't think he will shoot you. You keep talking about how paranoid Tuco must be. Have you listened to yourself lately?"

"Maybe he should be," Tuco said. "I'll shoot him if I have to, and maybe I will have to because he's come to kill me."

"Really," Lily said. "And he brought me along to watch? Whatever made you think so?"

"I got a note," he said.

"You got a fucking note," I said. But of course he did. From Milwaukee on hotel stationary. "You believed a note that says I want to kill you?"

"That's not what it said. The writer said one of us had to kill the old lady. He didn't know which one, but he knew who the CID would believe. You were the ex-cop. They'd believe you when you said you didn't do it. I'm the guy with old dope beefs. Why should they believe me? He said he didn't know which of us it was, but I would be better off if I hid. If you killed her you could claim I did, and you would get away with it, and if I killed her I might be dead meat anyway."

"Tuco," Lily called. "What made you think George killed her?"

"I knew he did," Tuco said. "It could only be one of the two of us and I knew it wasn't me."

I had been a fool. I've been a fool before, and I will be again.

"Lily, can tell you what I thought and why, " I said.

"He was sure it was you, Tuco, because he knew it wasn't him."

Tuco stepped out from the behind the rock. His fine hair was matted to his head with sweat. He had smeared dirt in his face to kill the shine of it. The rifle was still in his right hand, but the barrel was pointed at the ground barrel wavering. His left hand was trembling and tears were welling from his eyes. He had hiding hiding here for more than a month. His strain had been much greater than mine.

"We've been a pair of great fools," I said. "We should have talked, but I was afraid to. I was afraid I'd learn it was you."

"Me too," he said.

We wrapped each other up in a big hug and stayed there until Lily joined us and wrapped her arms around us both.

Slowly we disentangled ourselves. We walked up the road together, my arm around Tuco's shoulder, my hand around Lily's waist.

"We are friends," I said. "I may not believe in much, but I believe more than anything in us."

We were almost to the hall when there were more shots, but not from Tuco or me. Behind us there were a series of pops – not a rifle – but I knew the sound of the gun. The shooter didn't have our range. Dirt splashed up a good fifty feet behind us.

We made the corner of the building and around the back. I had never seen Lily move that fast.

Sometimes something weird happens in the middle of combat. You speed up so much that everything else seems to slow way down. I wasn't in the least frightened. I didn't have time to be frightened. Adrenaline surged through me not for fear but speed and exhilaration instead. I was probably moving very fast, but it felt like I was swimming through molasses.

Once we were inside, Tuco raced for a prepared position at the window. He had a sandbagged nest on a deal table, higher than the edge of the window, but deep enough in the room it was hard to see from outside in the shadow. He was in it now, scanning the approach to the building left to right and back again.

"Who the hell's shooting at us?" He asked.

"I'm guessing Hodiak. You know him. Ghost's lieutenant. I thought he might be following me on my drive up. There was a black Ford Mustang that we saw several times. I thought I'd lost him."

"What's he want?"

"Revenge. The way I took out Ghost spoiled his play for gang leadership."

"What do you want to do, Blondie?" Tuco asked.

"The usual," I said. "Draw him in, take him out of play, live to fight another day."

Tuco whooped. "How are we gonna do it?"

I made sure of the loaded clip and jacked a new live round into the chamber of my automatic.

"I don't think he's left the road," I said. "The road looks like our only way out, but we're not going down it. Give Lily your nest. If you keep your head down sweetie nothing will get you. Eventually Hodiak's got to come for us. When he comes we give him shots from the window to stall him, and then we fall back behind the building. You go right, Tuco. I'll go left. If he comes after me you follow him. I'll find cover and we'll have him between two fires. Same goes if he follows you."

"Take the rifle and take the window," Tuco said. "Let me load these magazines. I want to trade you gun for gun. You're a better rifle shot, and I've got a better weapon. My AR-15 is at my trailer if I can get to it. If he follows me we're going to come to the stream. I'll run up the creek. That will pull him up into a gully, and I know just where to get out. If you cross the stream before you follow, we'll both be above him and have him in a cross fire."

He'd reloaded the magazines for the rifle and ran toward me bent over to avoid being seen through the windows.

I caught the guy running toward us in Army camouflage, face paint, and a watch cap. He didn't have a rifle, but something shorter on a sling around shoulder.

I didn't have the rifle yet and he was well out of effective pistol range, but I still let loose three rounds to make him think about it. He made it to a small copse of trees about half his original distance to the building.

I had the spare magazine in my pocket. When Tuco came with the rifle we swapped.

Camo man tried to break from his trees, but I was pretty close to him with rifle fire and he got back.

I knew what the bastard was carrying when he raked the building with it, exploding planks and struts with the impact of the .45 caliber rounds.

"Grease gun," I yelled to Tuco. "Let's get out."

The M3A1 .45 caliber submachine gun, nicknamed grease gun, is a World War II vintage weapon with a slow rate of fire easily recognized. We had some off the books grease guns in Recon; I knew the sound. Hodiak could easily have plucked one or two from Ghosts' lost hoard.

Tuco and I bailed out the back as planned, running straight back a hundred feet. He yelled, "Break," and went right toward his trailer. I broke left and was quickly prone southwest of the building behind the trunk of a large cedar tree.

Tuco was shooting. Damn fool. Hodiak was shooting back. Maybe Tuco knew something I didn't. Or maybe he was just risking his ass. There was more cover from the brush wood than I had realized. I saw Tuco make the trailer, and I could see Hodiak following him.

I followed too, but very cautiously. Hodiak wasn't. He was intent on the trail of snaps, splashes, and gunshots that Tuco left him to follow. Maybe he had grabbed his AR-15, but Tuco was still shooting only pistol rounds. My job looked easy, but wasn't.

By the time I got to the creek, I could hear Hodiak splashing upstream, but I couldn't see him. I had to run to catch up, not an easy task at my age, but I did my best; afraid I might leave Tuco holding the bag, I ran up the hill on the far side of the creek ignoring the pain in my thighs and the stitch in my side.

I was well above and invisible to Hodiak now only a bit in front of me loudly splashing up the creek. I could walk now. I could see Tuco maybe a hundred fifty feet to my front. He was kneeling a bit behind some rock with his AR-15 at port arms. He pointed into the gully. I dropped prone at my edge and peered over.

Hodiak was taking a breather. He might have thought he'd lost us since he'd heard nothing from Tuco for a bit. He stood ankle deep in water with his hands behind his head breathing heavily.

Tuco laid down four quick shots, water splashed and bullets skittered wildly off the rocks.

"Drop the gun," he yelled, but he left off shooting too long, and Hodiak was now under cover from Tuco, crouched behind a man-sized boulder.

I had a pretty good feel for the aim of Tuco's rifle now. I picked a spot on the upper right edge of the right corner of Hodiak's boulder and scratched it with a shot.

"Drop it Hodiak," I cried. "I've got your back door. You've got no other choice but dying."

"Hold your fire. I'm giving up." He stood slowly with both hands raised and then, just as slowly, reaching across with his left hand, loosed the strap, and let the grease gun clatter into the creek.

Tuco pointed at me and then down, and took up his aiming position again. I ran, bounced, and slid down the side of the gully and into the creek still somehow keeping the barrel of rifle more or less pointed in Hodiak's direction.

The man in camouflage pulled off his watch cap with his left hand. When I saw Hodiak last his hair was fading strawberry red, but now it seemed quite rapidly become white.

Slowly, deliberately with our guns trained on him, he bent down to the creek, soaked his watch cap in it, and scrubbed off the camouflage paint.

"Who the hell is Hodiak?" The El Tee asked.

Tuco slid down into the creek. He didn't really look surprised. I was guessing, but pretty sure that Tuco and I both knew. After thirty five years we both had it figured out. I could hear him in my head, a memory of the night of pigs, often recalled, but never quite heard.

"You call it in, Rock," the El Tee told the Platoon Sergeant. "I'll be out on the line with the men."

In the confusion of random shots, claymores, and frags the El Tee had killed her and left Tuco and I damned for it.

CHAPTER 30

We bound the El Tee's hands with zip ties, loaded him in Tuco's pickup, and taking no chances, bound his ankles too. Tuco drove. I rode shotgun with my automatic in my hand, but pointed away for safety. Lily drove my Z3 down behind us.

For a while the El Tee chattered at us. "Won't do you any good. Your word against mine. You shot first."

Finally I held up the grease gun and asked, "Where the hell did you get this?"

"Same place you could. They were off the books in Nam. Not a part of our TO&E. I just mailed it home one piece at a time."

Tuco grinned, "I suppose that makes it legal?"

Then the El Tee shut up.

Tuco said there was probably a police station in Mt. Shasta, but he didn't know just where. "Probably Mt. Shasta Boulevard," he said.

As we rode down the hill I finally said, "I'm sorry, Tuco. I should never have doubted you."

"De nada," he said. "At least you didn't rat me out the way I did you."

"Rat me out?"

"I told Newton."

"I get it," I said. "You told him that the worst thing that happened in 'Nam was when your buddy murdered an old woman."

"I believed it at the time," Tuco said.

"So you had to get Newton away from Ghost. If Newton told that to Ghost, once the CID came calling, I'd be toast. Ghost would have owned me."

"That's right."

"Too bad you couldn't keep Newton alive."

"I tried," Tuco said. "He wouldn't listen."

"But he didn't talk. I saw his body. They did terrible things to him, maybe more painful than I can imagine, but afterward when I met Ghost he still didn't know."

"He always wanted to die some kind of hero," Tuco said.

"Your letter from Milwaukee, " I said.

"Yeah?"

"My guess is this bastard wrote it."

"Sure he did," Tuco said.

I jammed the automatic in the El Tee's ribs. "You're a real son of a bitch," I said. "Maybe I should just blow a hole in you now."

"Let it go, Duvall. He isn't worth it," Tuco said.

"Maybe not," I said, "but he ought to pay. Look what it cost us. Look who we might have been if we hadn't been living his lie, each of us always suspecting the other, each fearful of what the killing cost when all along it was a lie."

"But look what we got instead," Tuco said.

"What?"

Tuco smiled. "A brother," he said. "A friend who would gave his life for me as I would for him."

"You and me instead of you or me," I said.

"It's him not us."

"It's gotta be you," the El Tee said. "I am not that man. It's got to be him or you."

"We'll let you tell it to the judge," I said.

We didn't have to look very hard for the police station.

We drove up Lake Street past our motel, made the left turn on Mt. Shasta Boulevard and there it was. Lily parked the Z3 and said she'd take a walk.

The cop on the desk was in uniform. I showed him my badge. "This guy was trying to bushwhack me and my friend," I said, nodding my head in Tuco's direction.

"This bastard shot at me," the El Tee said.

"To defend my friend."

"He was out to bushwhack me," the El Tee said.

"If I had meant to whack you, you'd be dead."

"These two were trying to kill each other," the El Tee said.

"The CID will want him too." I handed the officer Elrond's card. "If he's not in his office, you can reach him on his cell."

The officer took a very long look at each of us. "Yup," he said. "Where did this happen?"

"The church camp up near Castle Lake. Tuco's been the caretaker there."

"Sheriff's jurisdiction," the uniform said. "You gentlemen can take it easy in our holding cells. I'll give him a call and see what he wants to do."

He took my automatic and the grease gun, and called in another officer to pat us all down. He took Tuco's knife, and the El Tee's folding tool. There were only two cells. He put the El Tee in one and me and Tuco in the other.

An hour or two later, a Sheriff's deputy arrived, an older man with thinning hair and belly threatening to jailbreak his belt. He spoke with the Mt. Shasta officer first and then interviewed us separately. Since the two he left could talk through our bars that wasn't the best procedure, but facilities were limited.

He talked to Tuco first which left the El Tee and me alone.

He turned his back on me and stood, hanging on the bars on the other side of the cage. His shoulders shook. I was surprised to discover I now felt sorry for him.

236

"Lawyer up," I said. "May be the best thing you can do. What reason could you have for this shooting at us today? I can't imagine how you can explain it. So maybe it's better if you don't.

"The evidence of our gunfight will be pretty clear, or it will be after Tuco and I have talked. They'll arrest you, but they'll never prove the other. It's been too long and nobody cares."

"The Army cares," he said. "You care."

"I only care that Tuco didn't do it" I said. "Why should I give a damn that you did? And how's the Army going to prove a thirty year old crime without a body or forensics? There's no proof. They've just got prejudices and opinions. Yeah I've got one too. I think you killed her, but I didn't see you do it."

"I can't be that man. That's not who I am. Maybe I have to prove it."

"You keep saying. What's it matter? I know who you are and I don't care. I just want you off my back. I'm sorry the old woman died, but I know I didn't do it. I know now that Tuco didn't do it. What's done is done. You can't undo it. What's it matter that we think you did it? Can't you live with that?"

He spoke no more and still would not face me. Shame, fear, pain, or grief, I could not know exactly what he felt. He was alone and would remain so until the deputy came to question him.

"How did it go," I asked Tuco.

He shrugged. "Who can tell? Mostly he asked the details of our little comedy. He asked me why I was sure you didn't kill the old lady, and he asked me why I was so sure the El Tee did."

"He didn't ask about the scene of the ambush?"

"Not much. He had photographs. He's been up there. Says he found a black Mustang that must be the El Tee's car. I think the physical evidence tells its own tale. He was trying to look at motives. He had an awful time trying to figure out how we could go through Vietnam but never talk about it."

"He looked old enough," I said. "But maybe he didn't serve. Maybe he has no idea what it was like when we first got back."

"What do you think is going to happen?" Tuco asked.

It was my turn to shrug.

"Think the CID will be hot for him?"

"We'll see," I said. I still didn't think Elrond was a real cop.

Finally it was my turn.

There's no point to recounting my interview blow by blow. I kept calm and told the truth, the whole truth, but nothing elaborate. My story pretty much told itself, and I didn't need to sell it. I was sure the El Tee had tried to sell his pretty hard.

Afterward the deputy brought us lunch, sandwiches without utensils, with water and coffee in paper cups. Tuco had managed to eat a full breakfast; I was famished, but tried to eat slowly. The El Tee wolfed his quickly.

About two the deputy came back with the Mt. Shasta cop. They unlocked both cells and opened the door.

"Gentlemen, please follow me. The City of Mt. Shasta has graciously given the use of the Chief's office as a conference room."

Two vertical file cabinets, a book case with glass doors, and a small typing table lined the walls. Family pictures were on one side of the large clean desk. A computer sat on the other side next to a telephone and a star shaped device I recognized as a speaker phone.

The deputy took the seat behind the desk. The rest of us, including the Mt. Shasta cop sat down in guest chairs facing him.

"That's a speaker phone," the Deputy said. He looked at me. "We've got Major Elrond on the line, and I'd like to hear from him first. Major would you please tell these gentlemen about the results of your investigation."

"Certainly," said Elrond through the loudspeaker. "My investigation is complete and so is my report. My Colonel is pleased with my work, and the Vietnamese diplomat is pleased too, according to our State Department liaison."

"You've already told me," the Deputy said. "Would you please repeat your conclusions for the other gentlemen here in my office?"

"Certainly. We have confirmation from 90 percent of the known members of the platoon where the death occurred. We found no evidence of foul play. All of them to a man say they think she was most likely killed by incoming enemy fire. The investigation is closed."

Slack mouthed, the El Tee stared at the speaker phone.

I smiled. "This is Duvall, Major. Congratulations on the whitewash. Would it matter to you if I said I lied?"

"That's my final report, Duvall."

"Thank you, Major," the deputy said. "We won't take up anymore of your time."

The deputy pushed a button and the line went dead. He carefully moved the photographs from the corner of the desk. He leaned back in the swivel chair and put his hands behind his head, propping his right leg over the vacant corner.

"Let's talk about the fun you boys have been having. Apparently this is all about who killed an old lady in Vietnam, but the Army thinks nobody did."

"She is dead," Tuco said.

"Has been for some time," the deputy said, "and meanwhile you fellas have been messing yourselves, pissing in the wind. It's official. Nobody did it. It don't mean nothing. Fortunately nobody got hurt."

"It don't mean nothing?" Tuco said. "You were in the Nam."

"Uh huh. 101st Airborne."

The El Tee looked a little green. He was staring at his hands, his mouth open, trying to breathe evenly.

"I could hold you all for assault" the deputy said, "but I don't see the point. What would be the good of it?"

"Maybe it could keep us from getting killed," I said. "This man tried to kill us."

"I think you're pretty safe. After the stories I've heard from you three today, I'm sure he knows who I'd come looking for if something happened to either of you. But why should it come to that?"

Tuco smirked. "You mean why can't we all just get along?"

"Uh huh."

"What about the grease gun?"I asked. "That is an illegal weapon without a special license."

The deputy reached in his pocket, pulled out a dollar bill and handed it to the El Tee. "We've got a no questions asked gun buy back program here in the county; I want to thank you for turning this in."

The El Tee looked stunned..

"Come on," said the Mt. Shasta uniform, "I'll write you a receipt." He grabbed the El Tee's elbow with his left hand and took him out of the room.

"You're not doing him any favors," I said nodding in the direction of the El Tee. "He needs his come to Jesus moment or he's never going to get over this."

"If I had to guess," the deputy said, "nobody can punish him any worse."

"Are we free to go?" Tuco asked. "I gotta get out here."

"Give us another moment, Tuco. We're free for the first time in years," I said. "But I'm going to take out little insurance policy.

"When the uniform brings him back, tell him Recon's going to know. You can thank him for all the names he's dug up. I'm going to tell them the whole damn story. He keeps saying that he can't be that man. I think I can make it clear at least to the guys who have a right to know that he's guilty as hell. Tuco and I aren't.”

"I'll tell him. He's guilty all right, but maybe not of a crime. Your problem is you think somebody gives a shit. Are you sure of what you would have done if you had to make his choice?"

"Yeah. I made it. So did Tuco. We risked our lives."

CHAPTER 31

After all those years Tuco moved out. He lives with Teri in her Petaluma house.

We still go to group sometimes. We've told them all about the El Tee. Group has changed.

I don't worry about Hodiak. I just carry my gun. I've got into the new habit of living a whole life.

Sometimes the only way out is through; some make it; and some don't.

Over coffee I told the story to Vinny. I suppose he told the other guys in El Sobrante. Dornacker was intrigued and looked into it. One afternoon he brought me a copy of a Milwaukee police report.

The television was still on, tuned to the one of the shopping channels when they found him. Little remained of a bottle of vodka found at the scene.

I guess the El Tee needed it to find the guts to eat his gun.

The invitation was formal, letterhead on heavy paper, but vague; I was invited to meet an official at 10 o'clock in the morning. I tried to dress accordingly.

I wore pleated wool trousers, a light blue dress shirt with a red and blue striped tie, and a blue blazer. I don't have a suit anymore. Usually I wear walking shoes or trainers. Today I wore my remaining pair of Ecco oxfords.

Lily dropped me at El Cerrito B.A.R.T. I transferred to Muni and got off the 47 bus at Van Ness and California. After a short walk and an elevator ride I found the Vietnamese Consulate on the 5th floor of 1700 California street.

I was greeted by a striking Vietnamese woman wearing a turqoise sheath. I showed her the invitation. After a few minutes she escorted me into a conference room. She indicated the coffee and tea service with a smile, and left me alone.

I helped myself to coffee. A small placard in English and Vietnamese indicated the coffee beans had been grown in the Vietnamese Highlands. I helped myself to fresh cream.

Suddenly he was there bowing. I didn't see him enter the room. I have no idea if bowing is a Vietnamese thing, but since I had fought only in the jungle and met few, the bow seemed appropriate.

I bowed back.

He wore a dark suit, white shirt, and a red tie. His shoes were polished to a mirror finish. He carried a manila folder under his arm.

"My name is Nguyen," he said.

"I am George Duvall," I said.

"I am pleased to meet you, Mr. Duvall."

"Likewise," I said.

"Undoubtedly," he said. "But please, let us make ourselves comfortable." His English was flawless but more British than American. He busied himself to make a cup of tea.

We sat in adjacent chairs, his at the head of the conference table, and mine just around the corner to his right.

"I think maybe your name was Nemesis," I said.

"Perhaps it was," he said.

"You're the senior official who insisted that a woman was murdered in my platoon," I said.

"I was."

"What's it matter now?" I asked. "The killer suffered enough and is dead by his own hand. What did it ever matter? It was war. People die."

"Please," he said. "She was my mother."

It's been more than forty years, but my memory of her is very clear, barefoot, skirts tied up to free her legs, and blood on her hands and chest. She didn't look remotely like the polished gentlemen seated next to me at the table.

"Your mother seemed to be a primitive," I said. "You are not."

"She was always more than she seemed," he said. "She was a Christian. She excelled at the mission school. The priests managed to send her to University in Paris. She witnessed the Nazi occupation of France and witnessed some of their attempts to exterminate Jews. She believed the Degar would be similarly destroyed if they did not achieve a separate country. She believed their best chance was the victory of Ho Chi Minh."

"The Degar?" I asked.

"You called us as the French did, Montangnards, people of the mountains."

"Nguyen is not a Montangnard name. You had your own language."

"True, but I was a war hero and I became an important part of the current regime. There are still many prejudices in my country. I found it politic to change my name."

"So you are a new Mr. Nguyen, and many, perhaps most, do not know that you are one of the mountain people."

"I am a changed man," he said. "But I'm still fighting the war of my youth and I'm still losing. The coffee you are drink is raised in our highlands. It is one of our most important cash crops. Every year we clear more jungles and plant more coffee. Where perhaps four million Degar lived in the highlands there are now only a million. I am grateful my mother did not live to see this."

"What made you believe she was murdered," I asked.

"Simple observation," he said. "Wounded her best hope of survival was to surrender to you, but she left me and others with clear orders. I drove the pigs at your perimeter to distract you. Others crept past your ambush on the other side of the trail and delivered our dispatches.

"None of us fired a shot, but in the morning she was dead. You did not leave her behind in the jungle as you would an enemy, but extracted her body as you would an ally, attributing her death to enemy fire. She was helpless. One of you shot her, perhaps as a precaution in your fear of the pigs, but certainly a result of cold calculation, but you treated her as if she was a casualty of the war."

"She was certainly that," I said. "So was her killer."

He opened the manila folder and pushed it toward me. The El Tee's obituary was clipped inside.

"In the beginning my lust for revenge was powerful but seemed futile. In middle age I was shocked to discover I had the means to seek it. As I grow older and watch the destruction of my mother's people, her war – our war – becomes more and more futile. In the end I encouraged your investigators to believe that perhaps she had died by accident. The chief investigator was happy to drop the case, but he passed on the report of your last skirmish."

He tapped the clipping in the folder. "This was not my wish," he said. "I regret this happened."

"Me too," I said.

"Do you regret the war?" he asked.

I shook my head. "How can you regret what makes you who you are?"

DISCLAIMER

The Last Lost Warrior is a work of fiction. If the characters are based on anyone they are each in their own way some aspect of myself. None of the characters should be confused with any other living person.

The events described do have some basis in reality. Most of the roads and businesses referred to did exist as described in 2006.

The police department of El Sobrante does not exist because, though a vital community, El Sobrante is not a city so much as a zip code. Parts of it are in the city of Richmond, parts in the city of San Pablo, and much of it unincorporated Contra Costa county. The illusion of a city is created by the map and roadsigns. I want to thank the residents for allowing me to create a fictional city there so Duvall could be their former police chief.

I almost certainly have misrepresented the law enforcement procedures in the town of Mt. Shasta. Those and any other errors are solely my own.

I am known among my friends to proudly be a veteran of Echo Recon, 1/7th Cavalry, 1st Air Cavalry Division during the Vietnam War. One of my oldest friends, Jinx McCombs, was one of the primary editors of the Warrior manuscript. She was acquainted with one of my vivid war stories from an account I shared with several people via email. She became concerned while reading the Vietnam flashback that perhaps in telling of this tale, I was exposing a real murderer.

I have rarely received so great a compliment on the quality of my story telling. Still I wanted to use the setting of a Recon platoon in salute to my comrades. I just had to make clear it wasn't 7th Cavalry - and it's not. The 7th Cavalry's pass phrase is always "Garry Owen" and not "Rogers Rangers."

I did base a good deal of the fictional incident on one real experience, but the murder was a quite deliberate fictional addition.

I knew I was telling a tale about Post Traumatic Stress Disorder, and I knew I would need an incident vivid and strong enough to haunt the lives of so many of my characters while still believable to those who had never served in combat.

Murder would work so I invented one from whole cloth.

There was never a wounded or unwounded native woman who was taken into the night perimeter of my Recon platoon. Certainly the 1/7th Cav may have participated in other atrocities but I personally know of none since they were slaughtered long ago at Little Big Horn.

Many of us were fully aware of Lt. Calley's trial at Ft. Benning and we were scrupulously trying never to kill anyone who was not also trying to kill us.

There is an incident in Warrior that I will proudly tell you is pretty plainly based on fact. There was a day when well over a hundred Montagnards walked into Recon's ambush, and a single soldier stepped out before them at the risk of his life. If the enemy had also been there, he would have died. Since the enemy was not there, no one died, and we were able to evacuate a great many natives from the war zone.

I think I know which man took that step. He has been scrupulous not to claim credit for it, and many who followed him now believe that perhaps they were the first. I'll leave him his anonymity. He certainly did not murder anyone.

The Last Lost Warrior is a work of fiction.

ABOUT THE AUTHOR

Tom A Preece graduated from Raymond College, University of the Pacific in 1967. He had been pursuing a Master's Degree in English Literature at U.O.P and protesting against the Vietnam War when he was drafted in 1969.

Assigned to the Infantry he postponed the inevitable on the job training in South Vietnam, by volunteering to be trained to become a Non Commissioned Officer, a so called Shake N Bake instant Sergeant. He graduated that school at Ft. Benning as a Staff Sergeant E-6 with an 11F, (Operations and Intelligence) military occupational specialty. In July of 1970 he proudly served in E Recon 1/7th Cavalry, 1st Air Cavalry Division. He ended his tour and military service in 1971.

Before and after his military service Mr. Preece enjoyed a number of temporary jobs, dish washing, driving a delivery truck, cab driving, radio advertising sales, even surviving briefly on poker winnings.

On a lark he took the federal Civil Service exam and was offered a position with the Veterans Administration, now the Department of Veterans Affairs. For thirty years he worked there with and for his fellow veterans until his retirement in 2007.

35779046R00152

Made in the USA
Columbia, SC
27 November 2018